BUILDING THE
P-40 WARHAWK

GLEN PHILLIPS AND KEVIN HJERMSTAD

KALMBACH BOOKS

From Kevin Hjermstad:
To mom and dad, who support and encourage all my endeavors.

From Glen Phillips:
To my late father, who got me started on modeling,
my mother, with whom I share a love of history,
and my wife, Rebecca, who actively supports both.

ACKNOWLEDGMENTS AND CREDITS

Few authors gather historical data alone. We are no exception. The following organizations and individuals contributed time and effort to make this book a reality.

Champlin Fighter Museum, Mesa, Arizona
Curtiss Wright Historical Society, Torrance, California
San Diego Aerospace Museum, San Diego, California
Yanks Air Museum, Chino, California

Stan Hoefler
Ray Wagner
Byron White

THE MODELERS
Kevin Hjermstad
Mark Marez
Tom Neely
Glen Phillips

All photos by the authors unless credited otherwise.

Printed in the United States of America

First printing 1997

For more information, visit our website at http://www.kalmbach.com

ISBN: 0-89024-565-7

Book design: Kristi Ludwig

CONTENTS

Introduction 4

1. P-40 History & Development 5

2. The P-40 in Detail 11

3. A Brief Review of Tools, Materials, and Techniques 20

4. Flight School: Building an Out-of-the-Box P-40E (✦) 24

5. Pacific Heavy Metal (✦✦✦✦) 27

6. Exterior Colors and Markings 32

7. Northern Exposure (✦✦✦) 44

8. The Flying Tigers (✦✦✦✦) 48

9. A Yank in the RAF (✦✦✦✦✦) 53

10. Warhawks Down Under (✦✦✦) 60

11. Operation Torch (✦✦✦) 67

12. South Africa in North Africa (✦✦✦✦) 73

13. Pacific Pink (✦✦) 78

14. Last of the Line (✦✦✦✦) 82

Index 88

AUTHORS' NOTE: The ✦ symbols above represent difficulty ratings for each project. Each rating takes into account the basic fit and engineering of the kit, as well as the fit between the kit and the after-market detail and conversion parts, if any. We also factored in the type of scratchbuilding supplies, if any, as well as the types of tools required. These ratings are meant as a general—and very subjective—guideline for you. If you begin with the easiest skill levels and work toward the more difficult, you will acquire skills with each project which will make subsequent work easier, and which, we hope, will make you a better modeler.

INTRODUCTION

The Curtiss P-40 was the mainstay of the United States Army Air Corps fighter strength when the United States entered World War II. While there were more advanced designs in development, the P-40 answered the first call to arms. And it was the P-40 that stayed in the forefront of the conflict from beginning to end. In U.S. Army service, the P-40's guns were first fired in anger in Pearl Harbor.

Various models of the aircraft went on to serve in Europe, North Africa, the Aleutian Islands, the China-Burma-India Theater, and the Pacific. It not only provided yeoman service to the United States, but also to the Australian, British, Chinese, French, New Zealand, and Russian air arms as well.

In most technical comparisons to Axis fighters, the P-40 fell short. And yet in real wartime battles the P-40 often proved superior. Was it soundness of design? Pilot skill? Luck? Probably a combination of all three. The P-40 had a reputation for strength and the ability to absorb combat damage. But what made it durable also made it climb and maneuver like a truck. So while most enemy fighters were faster, the P-40's weight gave it excellent diving speed that combined well with its more than adequate battery of six .50 caliber machine guns.

So, where does this leave the modeler? Well served, we think. P-40 models have been around since plastic kits were first issued. Most, if not all, have been issued with a sharkmouth of some kind. P-40s and sharkmouths just seem to go together naturally. In the 1990s, Mauve, AMT/ERTL, and Hobbycraft have issued new P-40 kits. And the number of aftermarket parts and decals has exploded—a bonanza for P-40 enthusiasts.

After we briefly discuss the history and development of the P-40, we will focus on the building of the P-40 in most of its permutations, concentrating on the operational variants. We have included a series of detailed photos of restored P-40s to help you enhance your kits. We will use 1/72 and 1/48 scale kits.

We will use standard modeling tools, some elemental scratchbuilding and painting techniques, and some aftermarket accessories to produce an assortment of P-40 variants. And we're going on a world-wide tour—the models are camouflaged in a variety of WW II Allied colors and markings. By trying one or more of the techniques described in this book, you will improve your own skills. For some, this could simply be a drilled-out gun barrel and exhaust. For others, it could be replicating every little rivet on the cockpit floor. There is a little something for everybody.

1

P-40 HISTORY & DEVELOPMENT

The late 1930s were exciting times for aircraft designers and builders, because design and manufacturing technology had grown by leaps and bounds, much of it spurred on by looming war clouds in Europe and the Far East. The P-40 and its immediate predecessor, the P-36, were products of those times. Development of the P-36 began in late 1934. The aircraft later flew as part of a U.S. Army Air Corps (USAAC) competition to replace the Boeing P-26. Although Curtiss Aircraft Company's P-36 lost the competition to the Seversky P-35, there was sufficient interest on the part of the U.S. Army to warrant further development of the P-36. Apparently, the development was justified because the Army ordered more than 200 aircraft in the summer of 1937. Deliveries began in

the spring of 1938. Even as the P-36s were being delivered, however, foreign designs were proving superior. Among those were the British Hurricane and Spitfire, the German Bf-109, and the Japanese A6M Zero and Ki-43 Hayabusa. By the time the Germans invaded Poland in September 1939, the P-36 was no longer considered world class.

XP-40. The Curtiss Aircraft Company wasn't blind to the increasingly obsolescent design of the P-36. Even as they were being built and delivered to the Army (as well as to overseas customers), efforts were being made to improve the design. These centered on the use of an in-line, liquid-cooled engine versus the air-cooled radial. The first of these was the XP-37. This aircraft featured the wings and tail of the P-36 combined

with a radically redesigned fuselage housing an Allison V-1710 engine, a turbo-supercharger, intercooler, radiator, and pilot in that order.

There were problems. The development of the supercharger in the U.S. wasn't as far along as those overseas, so reliability was less than adequate. There were two primary reasons for this. Foreign governments, especially in Europe, tended to push technological development in the aircraft and aircraft-engine industries and provided much of the financial means to do so. And the U.S. aircraft-engine industry tended to concentrate on high-power, air-cooled radial engines. Even worse, the pilot was so far back along the fuselage, he couldn't see anything. Thirteen aircraft were ordered as YP-37s, but their development ended there.

The designer of the P-36, Don Berlin, suggested the mating of the Allison V-1710 engine with a basic P-36 fuselage. The goal was to add the engine while making as few changes as possible to the P-36. From the leading edges of the wings back, the P-36 airframe was essentially unchanged. Then the Allison engine was neatly faired into the fuselage. A carburetor air scoop was added to the top of the cowling and an oil-cooler scoop was added to the bottom. The radiator was given its own housing and moved to the bottom of the fuselage directly behind the wings.

The first flight was made in October 1938. The design showed promise so development continued for slightly more than a year. During this time they made numerous changes to the airframe to improve performance. The single greatest change was moving the radiator to a chin position under the nose. Apparently engineers believed that its lower fuselage position made it too susceptible to damage. This theory was later disproved when the old design was used on the North American P-51. (The Hurricane, Spitfire, and Bf-109 also had radiators mounted in lower fuselage positions with no negative consequences.) The XP-40 finally met all of its design goals in December 1939 and production commenced in March 1940.

P-40. Even as the P-40 went into production, detail design changes were made. Most of these were to improve performance or maintainability. Revisions were made to the landing gear, exhausts, oil and engine cooling systems, carburetor intake, and fuel system. The P-40 was equipped with two .50 caliber machine guns in the nose synchronized to fire through the propeller. These aircraft lacked pilot armor, armored windscreen, and self-sealing fuel tanks, which would seem to be odd omissions considering what was going on in Europe at the time.

Two hundred P-40s were delivered to the USAAC by September 1940. The remaining aircraft on the contract were allocated to the French. These aircraft were later claimed by the

Fig. 1-1

Fig. 1-2

British Royal Air Force (RAF) when France fell to the Germans. These exported aircraft were also equipped with two .30 caliber machine guns in each wing. Most of the initial batch of aircraft going to the Royal Air Force wound up as advanced fighter trainers or reconnaissance aircraft since their lack of armor and self-sealing fuel tanks made them unsuitable for combat against Luftwaffe fighters. These aircraft were designated by Curtiss as the Hawk 81A-1 and the RAF as Tomahawk I (opening photo, figs. 1-1, 1-2).

P-40B. Considering all of the changes, Curtiss and the USAAC apparently skipped the "P-40A" designation and went straight to the "B" model after its next redesign. The P-40Bs were given armor and self-sealing fuel tanks to bring them up to the combat standards of the time. A .30 caliber machine gun was added to each wing to augment the two .50 caliber

weapons in the nose. The aircraft used the same Allison V-1710-33 "C" series engine as the P-40 so the weight increase meant decreased performance. The P-40B was the first model deployed overseas with squadrons going to Hawaii and the Philippines. More than 130 P-40Bs were produced for the USAAC before further modifications lead to the P-40C.

P-40C. The P-40C was the next variant off the assembly lines with deliveries commencing in April 1941. Apart from having a new fuel system, the P-40C could carry on its centerline an external 52 U.S. gallon fuel tank, which could be dropped in flight. These aircraft were also equipped with two .30 caliber machine guns in each wing. Nearly 200 aircraft were delivered to the USAAC and more than 900 were earmarked for delivery to the RAF, some of these being left over from the initial French order. Re-allocated from RAF stock

Fig. 1-3

Fig. 1-4

appeared. Aside from some minor aerodynamic improvements, the single greatest change was the provision for an additional .50 caliber machine gun in each wing. This gave the P-40E an impressive battery of six machine guns at a time when many nations were still using rifle-caliber machine guns. The P-40E was also given the capability of carrying six light (20-pound) bombs under the wings.

More than 2,300 P-40Es were built and allocated to the newly named U.S. Army Air Forces (USAAF), the RAF, Russia, and Australia. The P-40E was also the first model to be officially named by the USAAF; they named it the Warhawk. The RAF designated it the Kittyhawk I. Overall, the P-40E was slightly faster than the earlier P-40B/C, had heavier firepower in terms of guns and bombs, and had the ability to absorb more combat damage as a result of a stronger, heavier airframe. On the down side, the increased weight meant the climbing and turning abilities were inferior. The improved power of the new Allison engine also resulted in some minor directional instability. Many of the later-production P-40E-1 series had the leading edge of the vertical fin moved slightly forward and a fillet added to its base. Some sources have stated the fin and rudder were modified; however, a review of the aircraft parts catalog has revealed that this is not the case. Only the fixed vertical fin was changed; the rudders remained the same. While the increased side area helped, there was a more lasting fix down the road. As a side note, many of these later E-1s were used as advanced fighter trainers in the U.S. and never saw combat overseas.

P-40F (fig. 1-4). The P-40F was an effort on the part of Curtiss to improve the aircraft's high-altitude performance. A P-40D airframe was mated to a Rolls-Royce Merlin engine with a single-stage, two-speed supercharger and designated the XP-40F. A subsequent YP-40F was given a Packard-built Merlin V-1650 series engine. This was the same series engine used in the North American P-51B and later Mustangs.

were 100 aircraft going to China, where they formed the core of the American Volunteer Group (AVG)—the famed "Flying Tigers." An additional 200 airframes from the RAF went to Russia, which by this time (summer, 1941) was at war with Germany. The export aircraft were known as Hawk 81A-2, while the RAF designated them the Tomahawk IIA and IIB (the "B" could carry the drop tank.)

Note that between the P-40, P-40B, and P-40Cs built by Curtiss for the USAAC, as well as aircraft built for lend-lease or those contracted for directly by foreign governments, there was a blurring of some of the aircraft's identities. An aircraft started as a P-40 might have parts from the later P-40B or C when finally turned over to foreign governments.

P-40D/E (fig. 1-3). The P-40D, or Hawk 87A-1 as Curtiss called it, experienced the first radical change in

the basic P-40 design—the Allison V-1710-39 "F" series engine was added. And the contour of the nose forward of the wings was changed. A new and deeper radiator was moved forward, the nose guns were deleted, and the two .30 caliber guns in each wing were replaced by two .50 caliber weapons. Re-contouring the nose also meant some changes to the upper portion of the fuselage decking, which resulted in a new, though similar, windscreen and canopy. Other changes included increased ammo storage, hydraulic gun chargers, provision for a centerline 500-pound bomb in lieu of the drop tank, modified landing gear, additional fuel capacity, and pilot armor.

As improved as the aircraft was, fewer than 50 were ordered by the USAAC and RAF combined. No sooner had the testing on this model been completed when an improved version, the P-40E (Hawk 87A-2),

Fig. 1-5

Fig. 1-6

The new engine used an updraft carburetor instead of the Allison's downdraft carburetor, so the upper carburetor scoop was eliminated. The two circular radiators were changed to a single rectangular design. Two small circular oil coolers were used in lieu of the single large oil cooler used on the P-40E. The radiator scoop was moved slightly forward and deepened to incorporate a new carburetor scoop. The carburetor intake ducting ran between the two oil coolers. The P-40F now had a noticeably different nose profile. In addition to the improved performance, the P-40F was also able to carry a larger drop tank and bomb load. Internal fuel was also marginally increased. The six .50 caliber wing guns were retained.

As previously stated, the improved power of the P-40E resulted in some minor directional instability. The situation wasn't helped by adding a Merlin with even more power. To counter this effect, Curtiss lengthened the aft fuselage, which moved the verti-

cal fin and rudder further aft and put the rudder into a position behind the horizontal stabilizer. This change was incorporated on all late-production P-40Fs. More than 1,300 P-40Fs were built for the USAAF, British Commonwealth of Nations (as Kittyhawk II), and Russia. A few were provided to the Free French in North Africa (where

two pilots promptly defected to Vichy France with their new airplanes).

P-40K (figs. 1-5 and 1-6). The P-40K was essentially an E model with a newer, more powerful Allison V-1710-73 engine. Again, the increased power had an effect on lateral stability. The effect was apparently most pronounced on take-offs and landings. The extended

Fig. 1-7

Fig. 1-8

The RAF designated the P-40K the Kittyhawk III.

P-40L. By the time the P-40L appeared, the writing was on the wall at Curtiss. Other U.S. manufacturers were producing the P-38, P-47, and P-51. In one form or another, all of these were in operation and had combat experience. Furthermore, these designs had more potential for development than the P-40. The P-40L was essentially a P-40F with one important difference. In the ever-increasing effort to wring more performance out of the design, Curtiss tried to lighten the airframe. They removed one gun from each wing and internal items such as armor and reduced fuel capacity. Ammunition for the remaining guns was also reduced. The improved performance was found to be marginal at best and many of the items (such as armor) were put back on.

The 50 L-1s built had the short fuselage of the early F, while the later 650 L models had the long fuselage. These aircraft also had two-gun wings.

vertical fin and fillet used on the E-1 was added to the K-1 and K-5 series. Some photos of aircraft with this fillet are often labeled Ks, but the only way to really tell is to check the serial number. Later production runs of the K used the extended fuselage of the later series Fs. Of the 1,300 K models produced, about three-fifths had the short fuselage and extended fin/fillet variant.

The P-40L was the last of the Merlin-powered P-40s, since Merlin production was now allocated to the P-51. As the Merlins in the F and L models became worn out, they were re-engined with Allison engines and redesignated P-40R. Most P-40Ls were built for lend-lease customers.

P-40M. The P-40M was a derivative of the late-production P-40K and first appeared in November 1942. The main change was the installation of the more powerful Allison V-1710-81 engine. This engine was also used in the P-51A. There were other minor detail changes such as the addition of a rectangular air inlet on either side of the cowl behind the spinner and landing gear indicator pins that popped up from the wing surface to let the pilot know the gear was down and locked. The six gun armament was retained. Additionally, these aircraft were built with the long fuselage of the late-production Ks. The entire production run of 600 aircraft was slated for RAF use (as Kittyhawk III), however the USAAF operated at least one unit in China and another in the Solomon Islands in 1943.

P-40N (figs. 1-7 and 1-8). This was the end of the operational line for the P-40 series. The P-40N first appeared in March 1943. The first 400 aircraft were almost identical to the later P-40Ms with the exception of having four wing guns. This and changes to the airframe were to improve performance, especially at higher altitudes, by lightening the aircraft. There were nine batches of P-40Ns incorporating changes to fuel tanks and fittings, armament, engines,

Fig. 1-9

radios, canopies, the oil and engine cooling systems, etc. Block-20 aircraft and onward switched to the Allison V-1710-99 engine, but the last 220 built were given a V-1710-115.

Externally, the single greatest change was the new canopy arrangement. The fuselage area directly behind the cockpit was modified and a simpler rear canopy was installed. The pilot's sliding canopy was also changed and some of the frames behind were eliminated. The net effect was vastly improved visibility. The N was the most popular of the series with more than 5,200 of all variants built. Many went to the Far East where they served with the RNZAF (Royal New Zealand Air Force), RAAF (Royal Australian Air Force), RAF, and USAAF. The RAF designated the P-40N the Kittyhawk IV.

XP-40Q (fig. 1-9). The XP-40Q was a last ditch effort by Curtiss to further improve the aircraft and maintain pro-duction. The effort was partially successful in that the aircraft was much improved over its predecessors; however, it still wasn't better than the P-51s and P-47s already in production. After going through a few permutations, the single prototype ended up as arguably the most attractive of the series. The rear fuselage was cut down and a sliding bubble canopy was fitted. The entire nose was modified as well. The chin scoop was dramatically reduced and cooling scoops were added just outside the landing gear pods on the newly clipped wings. The new Allison V-1710-121 engine drove a four-bladed propeller, making this the fastest of the P-40 series. In late 1944, Curtiss discontinued development and production of the P-40 line. A total of 13,700 P-40s, in all its variations, had been built. The sole P-40Q ended its days as a racing aircraft and was destroyed in a crash.

2

THE P-40 IN DETAIL

This is the instrument panel of a P-40B.

On the left side of P-40B cockpit, notice the throttle quadrant, fuel selector control, rudder-elevator trim, cockpit light, rudder pedal, and electrical box. The predominant color of P-40 cockpits was ANA 611 Interior Green and the instrument panels were black. *Curtis Wright Historical Society (CWHS)*

Modeling is often about details. Whether reproducing a shape or a color, you are trying to replicate a physical object in miniature. Most reference material provides only a portion of what you need. It always seems to lack a key element or bit of information. This chapter is designed to fill in all the blanks and focuses on the areas of the airframe that are most visible on the completed model. These are the engine, cockpit, landing gear, flaps, and the belly tank mounts.

The information is divided by aircraft type—the P-40B, P-40E, and P-40N. The photos are from various aircraft—some operational and some restored museum pieces. Each photo and caption will provide information you will need to enhance any P-40 project. Where possible, we have noted the presence of non-standard equipment or colors, as well as missing equipment. The photos are taken so the subject, such as the landing gear, is shot from multiple angles. This will help you duplicate the real thing.

You can see the flap and landing gear control mechanism on the back left side of the P-40B cockpit. *CWHS*

Look for the rudder pedals, parking brake handle, gun chargers, and wing tank fuel gauge on the front floor of the P-40B. *CWHS*

This is the mid-wing section of a P-36 (Hawk 75) under construction. This section was identical to the early P-40s and similar to the later P-40D-N. You can see the flange bolting the wing together and the mounting point for the control stick. The aileron torque tube runs along the centerline and the elevator control rod is folded up forward. The hydraulic handpump is in the foreground. The curved brackets are the mounts for the fuselage fuel tank. The small brackets in front of the tank mounts are for the seat uprights. *CWHS*

The P-40 through P-40C used the Allison V-1710-33 "C" series engine. The gray and black colors shown are typical of the series. The V-1710-39 replaced this engine in the P-40D because of oiling problems inside the long reduction gear housing at the front of the engine.

The V-1710-33 used a Bendix-Stromberg downdraft injection carburetor and a single-stage supercharger. The power was adequate at low to medium altitudes, but it fell off at higher elevations. While this was consistent with U.S. government policies at the time, the RAF used the aircraft as a low-level recon or Army Cooperation Command asset.

The supercharged fuel-air mixture ran into the intake manifold, where it was fed into the cylinders.

The two radiators and single oil cooler were mounted below the engine. Air entering through the chin scoop passed through the coolers and out the back of the cowling via four variable cowl flaps. The radiators were a natural metal color. *CWHS*

This view of the canopy of the P-40B shows the canopy track and interior windscreen armor. This style of canopy track was used on the P-40 through P-40C. The earlier P-40 lacked the windscreen armor. *CWHS*

The lower panel of this P-40E instrument panel is painted green, although lower panels were usually black.

This rear view of the left cockpit side shows the map light and landing gear-flap control system.

The left cockpit side shows the throttle quadrant, trim controls, and fuel selector control. The throttle quadrant linkages and a rudder cable are also visible. The black panel and dial in front of the stick are a modern addition.

On the right side of the cockpit you can see the canopy crank, cowl-flap control, electrical boxes, and hydraulic pump (with a non-standard handle). The silver box aft of the canopy crank is in the normal position of the oxygen regulator.

The right side of a different P-40E shows the oxygen regulator, wing fuel-tank gauges, hydraulic pump and associated plumbing, rudder cable, and elevator control horn behind the seat. Note the wear pattern on the cockpit floor.

Early P-40s used a ring-and-bead gunsight and later P-40s carried an internally mounted N3 reflector gunsight. The N3 sight could be equipped with a crash pad and a gun camera.

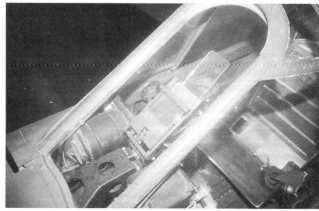

P-40s used a number of different seats, some made of wood, but most made of stamped metal as shown here. Some had round backs, while others were squared. The deep seat pan housed the pilot's parachute. We removed the armor plate to provide a limited view into the aft fuselage. Also visible are the elevator control horns and tube running behind the seat.

This view shows the armored glass and gunsight reflector glass. The upper instrument panel was usually covered with a black shroud. The armor glass, 1.5" thick, was built into the frame.

This view of the aft cockpit area shows the pilot's headrest and the seat mount. The seat could be adjusted vertically, sliding up and down the mounting tubes.

This is another style of seat mount that may be non-standard. Note the different headrest.

The external sills of the open canopy reveal the canopy track and cable used to open and close the canopy. This arrangement was used on P-40D through P-40N.

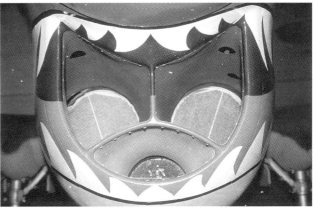

Down the mouth of the beast. Internal shrouds ducted air into the radiators (upper) and the oil cooler (lower).

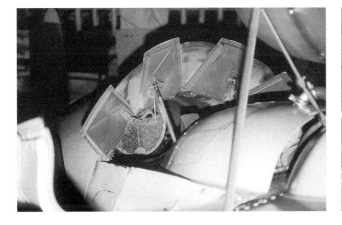

Air left the radiator-oil cooling bay via four variable exit cowl flaps, which had a small sub-flap between them that closed the gap as they opened. Note the small linkages that are visible on fully opened flaps.

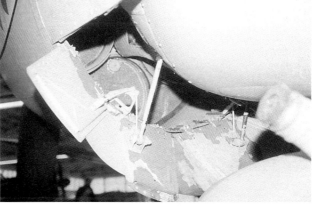

Here's a view of the cowl flaps from the other side.

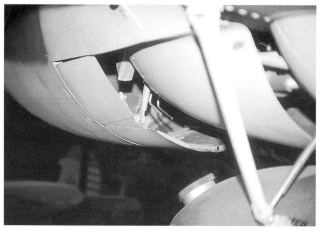

The cowl flaps in the closed position look relatively thin.

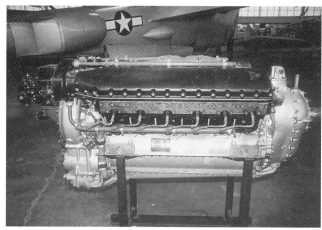

The Allison V-1710-39 "F" series engine was first installed in the P-40D. Later models of the P-40 used variations of this engine with a different dash-number.

The reduction gear housing was shortened in the P-40D, which led to an overall reduction in the P-40Ds length compared to the P-40 through P-40C.

The supercharger and carburetor setup was largely unchanged from the earlier -33 engine. However, engineers tweaked the carburetion, induction, exhausts, etc., to increase the power throughout the engine's life cycle.

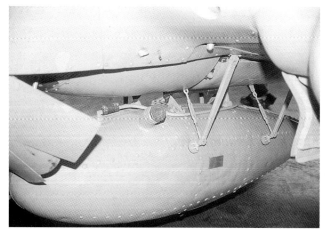

All P-40s from the C model onward had the capability to carry a releasable belly fuel tank. The tank was secured to the airframe via a small rack on the centerline and four sway braces. This style drop tank may not have been the standard installed on P-40s.

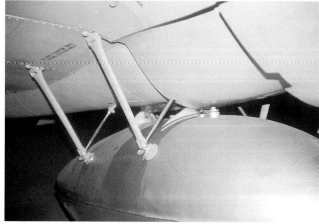

This style of drop tank on another P-40 is more common to the series. Also note a slightly different style of sway brace.

When you view the drop tank from the other side, the shallow pylon is barely visible.

In this view of the right wing flap and well, you can see the torque tube and rods.

The flaps and well were symmetrical. This is the inner portion of the left flap. The inner portion extends into the underside of the fuselage. Note the reinforcing plate in line with the wheel well. The plate is on both flap wells.

On the inner face of the flap, note the small notch that aligns with the reinforcing plate.

In this front view of the strut and wheel, note the routing of the brake line and the tow eye. Most early-production P-40s had smooth tires, but as the war progressed the tires typically had a diamond- or block-pattern tread. Additionally, all P-40s had a spoked wheel, which on the P-40 through P-40L was usually covered with an almost flush-fitting plate fastened with four bolts. Most photos of P-40Ns show the wheel without the coverplate.

From the rear of the strut you can see the torque link and the brake-line routing.

This view of the front wheel well shows the lightening holes and some minor plumbing. According to some sources, the wheel well was sometimes covered with a leather or canvas shroud.

This is how the brake line is attached to the hub. The tire with circumferential tread is a modern item.

The strut rested against the outer skin of the wing and was enclosed by a pod and two doors.

The tail wheel was completely retractable and covered by two flush-fitting doors, which were pulled closed by the two arms as the tail wheel was retracted.

The tail wheel was steerable via the rudder pedals. Note the doors do not hang vertically, but are splayed outward. The "V" antenna and its mount are a modern addition.

The instrument panel of the P-40N. Note the differences between this and the P-40E panel. The bottom panel/box is non-standard (arrow). The gunsight is missing and the cockpit is painted in a non-standard gray versus the regulation ANA 611 Interior Green.

The right cockpit sidewall. Again, generally similar to the P-40E. Note the addition of a carburetor air control handle in the upper left portion of the photo. P-40M and N aircraft were equipped with additional carb-filtered air inlets on both sides of the nose. The air control would open the auxiliary inlets and close off the ram intake on the top of the cowling.

The left cockpit side. The arrangement was generally similar to the P-40E. Note the additional kidney armor mounted on the sidewall next to the seat.

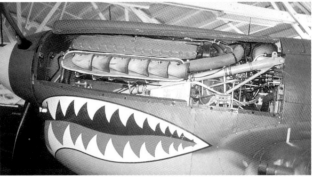

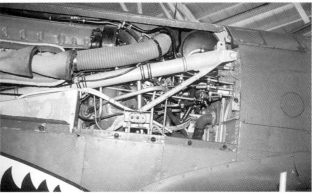

P-40Ns were usually equipped with a square back seat. The aircraft retains its armor plate. Visible are the control rods coming off the stick, the rudder cable on the left, and the gauge for the auxiliary wing fuel tank.

3

A BRIEF REVIEW OF TOOLS, MATERIALS, AND TECHNIQUES

For whatever reason, you like the ancient and honorable art, science, and skill of plastic aircraft modeling. That's why you're reading this book. You've gone beyond the "I built models when I was younger" stage and you want something more. Gone are the days when a model was built and painted over the course of a weekend, played with for a few weeks, and then forgotten or consigned to a junk drawer. We've all been there.

Over a period of time, your interest has matured. You've probably read some magazines and books on modeling and perhaps purchased or borrowed some reference material on a subject that interests you. If you haven't, this chapter will introduce you to some basic modeling tools and materials—some "must haves" and some "nice to haves." This chapter will also explain how to use these tools and materials. If you've already got the tools and know how to use them, then you can use this chapter as a review.

Basic tools. Basic tools are the ones you must have and are those you will use for about 90 percent of your modeling. These items are listed below.

> Hobby knife and knife blades
> Files: round, flat, triangular, half round
> Tweezers
> Sanding sticks (various grits)
> Sandpaper or sanding film (various grits)
> Clamping devices
> Masking tape (low-tack)
> Scissors
> Draftsmen's ruling pen or "0" brush for applying liquid cement.
> Paintbrushes (assorted sizes)
> Airbrush and air source

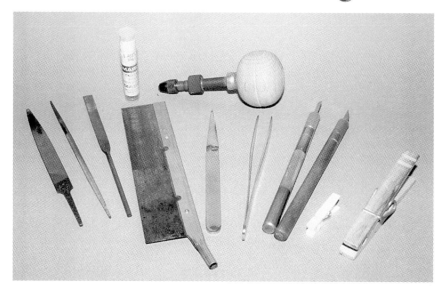

The expanded toolbox. You will find that as you get better at modeling and start adding more details, you will find yourself looking for different types of tools to either save time or complete a difficult task. And further down the modeling road, you'll probably find yourself making your own tools as well. For this you'll need:

> Sprue cutters
> Razor saw and miter box
> Pin vise and miniature drill bits
> Riffler files
> Sub-miniature punch set
> Motor tool and bits
> Scriber
> Panel line templates
> Super-glue applicator
> Putty spatula
> Miniature bench vise
> Photoetched miniature shears

Fillers. Fillers are used to fill seams and cracks, sculpt new shapes, etc. There are a wide variety of fillers ranging from those made specifically for plastic models to those used for household and automotive repair. Super glues can also be used as a filler. All are useful, and most are perfectly adequate for their particular tasks. The fillers used in this book are those you can find in any reasonably equipped hobby shop. These are Squadron Green Stuff and White Stuff and Tamiya Putty. Common super glues include Zap, Duro, and Locktite.

Paints and brushes. The two basic types of modeling paint are acrylics and enamels. Acrylics are formulated to be thinned with water or an alcohol. Enamels use a petroleum-based thinner. Both come in a wide variety of colors and brand names and both are acceptable for painting models, although each has advantages and disadvantages compared with the other. Acrylics dry faster, are usually nontoxic, and can be cleaned off in the kitchen sink. Enamels tend to adhere better and come in a wider range of colors. Regardless of which you choose, in most cases it is best to use the manufacturer's thinner when airbrushing or mixing colors.

Model paints must be shaken or stirred thoroughly prior to use, especially if they have been sitting for a while. Many paint problems stem from the paint not being properly mixed. While many paints can be used directly out of the bottle for brush painting, almost all paints must be thinned for use in an airbrush. The ratios with which model paints are thinned varies from manufacturer to manufacturer. Often trial and error is the only way to discover the best mix for your particular airbrush setup. Acrylics can be cleaned with isopropyl alcohol purchased in a drug or hardware store, and enamels can be cleaned off with mineral spirits. You don't have to use your more expensive model paint thinner to clean your brushes and airbrush.

Another useful paint is artists' oil paint, usually available at craft or art supply stores. Oil paints are particularly good for making washes and as a mixing medium for drybrushing. Oil paints have advantages: they come in a wide variety of colors and they have a long working time. The most common oil paint colors in aircraft modeling are black, raw or burnt umber, and white.

Paintbrushes come in a wide variety of shapes, style, and prices. A typical general purpose assortment includes nos. 000, 0, 1, 2, and 3 round sable brushes with good points, a ¼" flat sable or camel-hair brush, and a stiff-bristled ⅛" to ¼" brush for drybrushing. Always buy the best paintbrushes you can afford. Good brushes are expensive but with proper care will last a long time. Cheap brushes do not last as long and can make your painting less enjoyable.

Brushes must be thoroughly cleaned at the end of each painting session. Round brushes should have their tips restored to a point after cleaning. It's a good idea to wash them in a mild soap and water solution to help restore the softness to the bristles after the paint has been removed with the chemical solutions. Always store brushes with the bristles upright. If a brush came with a protective sleeve for the bristles (common on finely pointed brushes), use it.

Airbrushes. There are a wide variety of airbrushes on the market from inexpensive plastic spray guns to pricey professional systems. Most airbrushes for modeling are moderately priced. The major choice you will need to make is between single- and double-action airbrushes. Single-action airbrushes have separate controls for regulating the amount of air and paint. Double-action airbrushes combine both these actions into one control. Testor's, Badger, and Paasche are the most common names for modeling airbrushes in the U.S. A simple Badger 150 or Paasche H are more than adequate for 90 percent of modeling airbrush requirements. Air sources range from disposable cans to silent compressors with their own built in tanks.

Detailing materials. Most modelers start building out of the box. However, after their first contest or model meeting, they realize there is much more they can add to their modeling efforts. Detailing will enhance or correct the basic kit. You will need styrene materials (rod, tubing, strip, and plastic sheet) or stretched sprue to compete these projects, because these materials can be used to duplicate almost any component. You can find preformed styrene shapes at any well-stocked hobby shop. You might also want to use wire, drinking straws, and pieces of brass or other soft metals. Plastic in disposable household items can also be used to replicate additional details on a model.

Aftermarket accessories. Because of the advances in resin and photoetching technology and an explosion in the aftermarket industry, we now enjoy a wealth of detail parts undreamed of ten years ago. You can fully detail a model without having to fabricate any components. So now you have a choice between fabricating your own components or buying aftermarket detail sets to enhance your models. The wide variety of resin and photoetched kits and accessories are available at well-stocked hobby shops that cater to the plastic modeler. And don't ignore the model railroad section of a hobby shop, either. Locomotive and rolling stock detailing parts can sometimes be useful when detailing model aircraft and armor projects. If you can't find what you need locally, there's always mail order.

One of the simplest ways to do something different is to purchase aftermarket decals. They are often a higher quality than those included with the kit. Also, kit decals are usually limited to one to three choices, while an aftermarket sheet might offer more than that. Camouflage patterns and colors, national insignia, and personal markings can all be changed. Many decal manufacturers also offer sheets of national markings, numbers, and letters to further broaden your choices. Personal markings, such as nose art, are up to the modeler. Some decal manufacturers market their own decal setting and softening solutions to help the decals conform to the model's surface.

Basic Techniques

Building an out-of-the-box model is one of the best ways to improve your skills. As much as you, flush with enthusiasm from the latest model contest or magazine article, might like to jump on a big, expensive, and time-consuming super project, you should ask yourself, "Am I ready?" The answer lies in your last project. Does it have seams or visible gaps, fogged clear parts, misaligned wings, splayed landing gear, paint drips, or silvered, peeling decals? If so, it's time for a brief review and practice of some modeling fundamentals. In the long run, you'll be a better and more satisfied modeler. You also get to make the contest judges work a little harder.

Seams. All models have seams. Whether they are mold seams or construction seams, they are there. Wherever two or more pieces of a mold come together, a mold seam is created. Some manufacturers are better than others at disguising them or keeping them to a minimum, but there will always be some and you will need to remove them. They are especially prominent on round section parts such

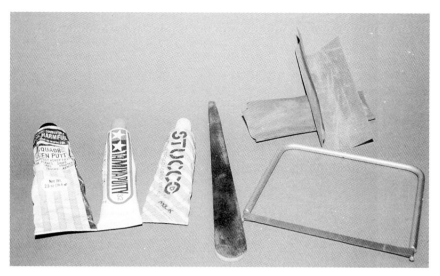

as gun barrels or landing gear struts. And remember, where there's one, there's usually another on the other side. Many mold seams can be easily removed by lightly scraping them with a knife blade. Others may require an assortment of files and sanding films.

Construction seams are the result of your modeling efforts. Wherever you join two parts there is a construction seam. Since real airplanes don't have a big seam on the fuselage centerline with little blobs of glue oozing out of it, neither should your model. As with the mold seams, some manufacturers are better than others at engineering a kit for proper fit. Oftentimes there is a relation between the fit and the price of the kit. Consequently, you can probably save a lot of grief by building well-engineered kits.

Woodworkers have a saying: "Measure twice, cut once." The sentiment is perfectly applicable here. Dry fitting the parts before you start cementing them together helps you identify and prevent problems. While test fitting you will find bits of excess plastic, warps, misaligned pins, or other things that could interfere with proper fit and alignment. Fix the problem before going any further. Once you're ready to cement parts together, take the time to put them in proper alignment and keep them there while the glue sets. Watch for construction seams that fall along natural panel lines. If the kit is well-engineered, this

may not be a problem. However, if the fit is less than perfect, you might have to remove the seam and then have to restore a panel line. Ultimately, careful fitting and assembly will go a long way in keeping post-assembly sanding and filling to a minimum. Then again, maybe you like sanding dust.

Basic Assembly: Most model aircraft kits follow a similar order during the assembly process: interiors, the fuselage and wings, landing gear, exterior details, clear parts, exterior painting, and decals. Detail painting is usually done during the individual assembly phases. There are exceptions, of course. For the most part, you can't go wrong by following the instructions. If you're new at modeling, you will want to follow the instructions until you develop your skills. If you've been at it for a while and have a number of models under your belt, feel free to deviate from the instruction sheet when time and your construction and painting methods warrant it.

Read the instructions before beginning any model. Decide what optional markings and parts (if any) you want to use before you start. If necessary, use a highlighter marker to flag those area of the instruction sheet indicating special construction requirements, such as pre-drilling a hole or selecting optional parts specific to the color scheme you've chosen. Take the time to familiarize yourself with the parts and their location on the

sprues as well. Every so often, the kit manufacturer will make a mistake on the instruction sheet. Most often, it's just a incorrect part number, such as labeling the left gear strut with the right gear strut's part number.

You might want to write down notes or create a checklist about the kit before and during construction. A checklist of things to do and when to do them is a great help when planning an out-of-the-box project or a major conversion. This is especially true if you tend to let your enthusiasm get the best of you. It happens to all of us. A list will help you stay on track and may help prevent mistakes.

Painting. There are two basic phases in painting a model. One is the detail painting, such as cockpit interior parts, which is done prior to or in conjunction with the assembly process. The second is the application of the exterior color scheme, whether by handbrushing or airbrushing.

Detail painting is fairly straightforward. A single part is usually painted a single color. If that's all you are doing, it's simple and relatively fast. If, however, you going to weather the aircraft, then it will take more time, because each layer of color must dry before another is added. For example, the basic color of a P-40 was Interior Green. The instrument panel, the control stick grip, and many of the component on the cockpit sidewalls are black. To enhance the shadows, you may add a wash. A wash is a mixture of about 90 percent paint thinner 10 percent paint. If the green and black paint on the cockpit parts isn't dry and hard, the wash is going to soften it and it will peel right up. The result will be an overall dark, soupy green mess. This is a good time for some minor deviations from the instruction sheet. While you are waiting for paint to dry, you can remove mold seams from parts. So, plan accordingly.

Painting the exterior is a little different. Most instruction sheets indicate that you should paint the exterior after the model has been assembled. We think it is best to paint the exterior after the main components of fuselage,

wings, and tail have been assembled, but before little things like propellers and landing gear have been added. If you paint the exterior last, you will have to mask parts off. Again, make these decisions before you start and plan accordingly.

Before you start painting, take a look at the model and make sure you haven't forgotten anything. The model's surface should be clean and free of grease and oil. You can remove oil by washing the model in warm soapy water with a toothbrush or by wiping it down with chemicals such as Polly S Plastic Prep. Use a tack rag to make a final wipe of the surface to remove any lingering dust. Work areas contribute to paint contamination too. A room inside the house is a lot more environmentally controlled then a dusty garage. Try to keep your model room clean and vacuumed. If you build models in the garage wet the floor (if possible) an hour before painting to keep down the dust. It's also a good idea to have a clean storage area, such as a clean box or a special drying cabinet, to place the model in while it is drying. Remember, some model finishes take more than 24 hours to dry.

Masking. There are a wide variety of masking mediums available—everything from special tapes to chemical masks which are brushed on, then lifted off when the painting is done. Try all of them and find what works best for your masking needs. Some combinations offer the best of both worlds, such as using 3M Fineline tape with Testor's Parafilm to fill the center section. The most important features of any masking medium is that it be low tack (won't pull up paint) and doesn't leave residue behind.

Paint Application. Paint is applied with two different tools—a paintbrush or an airbrush. An airframe can be painted with a hand brush, but the resulting finish is usually less then satisfactory. Most modelers begin using an airbrush early in their modeling careers. An airbrush is a significant expense for many modelers, but in the long run it will be worth it. The airbrush gives better coverage using less paint then hand-brushing. The airbrush will also paint the entire model more quickly than you can brush it by hand. Hand-brushing can leave brush strokes on the surface of the model, and some paint effects such as faded paint, forced panel lines, and natural metal can only be accomplished with an airbrush. Our advice is: invest in a high-quality airbrush and compressor, keep them clean and serviced, and they will give you a lifetime of use. You will need to practice using your airbrush because the more you use it, the easier it will be to use. You'll probably wonder how you survived without one.

Decals. All decals must be applied on a smooth surface. That is why you must spray a clear gloss onto a model prior to decaling. The decal will settle into the smooth finish. If you do not apply a gloss finish, air gets trapped underneath the decal and it will silver when it dries. To melt the decal into the paint, apply decal setting solution. This will assure that the decal bonds to the surface and that it won't wrinkle. You can also apply another gloss finish after the decals have dried.

Flat coats. One of the final steps in finishing your aircraft is applying the flat finish. Many types of paint are available in a flat finish. Acrylic, enamel, and lacquer have some sort of flat sealer-coat available. Many modelers apply flat coats of one type over other paint types, such as an acrylic flat over an enamel paint. Most model finishing systems seem to work well together. However if you plan to use two dissimilar materials, always pre-test them on scrap plastic before applying them to a model. Flat finishes can also be brushed on shiny spots to blend them into the paint.

Weathering. Aircraft spend most of their time outdoors. Combat aircraft, especially those in forward areas of a combat zone, usually do not have the luxury of hangars. They face the effects of nature daily. To make your model look more realistic, add gun and exhaust streaks, faded paint, oil and hydraulic leaks, and paint chips. You can artificially fade paint by mixing thinned and lightened paint. To create the effect of chipping, use paint and silver pencils. To darken the recesses of your model, you can apply a wash made with thinned paint. And to add highlights to raised details and the surface of the paint you can use a technique called drybrushing, which is almost the reverse of washing. To simulate dust and exhaust and gun streaks on the aircraft, you can airbrush it with thinned paint or apply chalk pastels.

For further reading on this subject see *Building Plastic Models* by Robert Schleicher, published by Kalmbach Publishing Co.

4

FLIGHT SCHOOL: BUILDING AN OUT-OF-THE-BOX P-40E

Model by Glen Phillips

For this out-of-the-box project we will use Hasegawa's P-40E in 1/72 scale. The kit is more than 20 years old but has withstood the test of time very well and is easily the best 1/72 scale P-40E on the market. The dimensions and shapes are basically accurate (few models are completely accurate), the fit is reasonably good, and it has engraved panel lines. The cockpit is rudimentary, containing only a floor, seat, stick, and instrument panel. The seat isn't accurate and the instrument panel is actually a decal. This level of detail was common at the time and, generally speaking, things haven't changed much in the last 20 years. Markings for this kit include an RAF Kittyhawk I in a desert camouflage scheme and a USAAF P-40E in olive drab and neutral gray. For simplicity's sake, we'll be going with the USAAF version.

Assembly. Every journey begins with the first step. In this case, step 1 is painting and assembling the cockpit components. Remove the cockpit components from the sprue and the mold seams where necessary. Cement the parts together and let them set up for a few minutes (fig. 4-1).

Paint the cockpit floor, seat, and stick Interior Green. We used Testor's Model Master Interior Green FS 34151. The instruction sheet suggested painting the cockpit side walls in step 5. But since you've already got the paint and brush ready, do the side walls in step 1. This saves time and brush cleaner. Paint the stick grip flat black as well as the instrument panel. The instruction sheet said to do it in step 3, but, again, your brush is ready now. Paint the seat belts a pale gray and the buckles a dull silver.

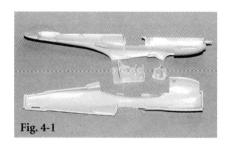

Fig. 4-1

In step 2 you will paint and assemble the radiator- and oil-cooler components. Two parts, two colors, too easy. Add a black wash to the base and interior of all three coolers.

Step 3 in the instructions said to paint and decal the instrument panel. Since you painted the panel earlier, and the paint dried, all that remains is to add the decal.

In steps 4 and 5 you get into the meat of the airframe, assembling the wings and the fuselage. Remove the parts from their sprues and clean off any remaining burrs. Carefully check the mating surfaces for any excess plastic, flashed-over alignment pin holes, and anything that will prevent a close fit. Dry-fit the parts together and look for any gaps, warps, or other distortions. Our kit had some ridges along the right wing tip, which forced the upper and lower halves apart. We made a few swipes with a fine sanding stick to remove the plastic. If you do find excess plastic, resist the temptation to charge in with coarse files or sanding film. You run the risk of removing too much plastic too fast.

Assemble the wing parts with liquid cement. Hold the parts together and touched the seam with a brush full of cement. The cement will travel along the seam. Lightly clamp the parts together for about 10 minutes. Don't clamp parts too hard or they may distort and dry in that position. Also, watch for liquid cement running out of the seam and under the clamping device. It will mar the finish and may glue a plastic clamp to the wing. For whatever reason, Hasegawa molded the inner portion of the flap onto the bottom wing, while the rest of the flaps are molded to the upper wings. Since the flap is one piece, take care to keep the flaps sections properly aligned. You will need to remove that seam later on. The more careful you are at aligning those pieces, the less work you will need to do on the seam later. Don't forget to remove the mold seam from the pitot tube on the left wing tip. When the wings are dry (gummy cement and plastic doesn't sand very well), lightly sand to remove the seam around the leading edge of the wing and the flaps. Use filler if necessary and sand again to make the seams invisible.

Assembling the fuselage halves is fairly straightforward, but may require a bit of manual dexterity. First dry-fit the parts and make sure there are no burrs or flash interfering with the fit. Take care of any potential problems with a light sanding and test-fit again. Continue to sand and dry-fit until the parts go together without any gaps.

Next, cement the radiator and oil-cooler assembly into the right fuselage half and then dry-fit the left fuselage half to the right again. Get everything lined up and then look down the intake throat. Make sure the radiator assembly is straight (isn't pointing to one side or the other) and isn't twisted inside the radiator bay. Lightly clamp the fuselage halves together for a few minutes while the radiator assembly dries. This technique can be used almost anytime you have to cement parts into one side of something before you attach the other side. It takes a little longer, but prevents other alignment problems.

In step 6 you will begin the detail assembly and put the main fuselage and wing components together. Since the fuselage isn't quite finished yet, you can remove some of the detail parts from the sprue, clean off the mold lines (don't forget the edges of the horizontal stabilizers), and assemble the bomb or drop tank. When you finish this, return to the fuselage in step 5.

The radiator should be fairly well set in place. Cement the fuselage halves together and once again, lightly clamp them in place. When they are dry, lightly sand the seam along the top and bottom. Pay particular attention to the base of the right side of the vertical stabilizer. Fill gaps if necessary. Alternatively, use a bit of gap-filling super glue and sand it down within a couple of minutes. This seam falls on a natural panel line, so you must restore it with a light scribing (fig. 4-2).

When the fuselage is reasonably dry, add the previously painted and decaled instrument panel from the underside of the fuselage per the kit instructions. As with the radiator, make sure the panel is properly aligned. Insert and cement in place the remaining cockpit assembly from step 1 Again check the alignment. If the seat appears tilted to one side or the other, make the necessary adjustments.

When the individual wing and fuselage components are completed, you can dry-fit them, check the alignment, clean the mating surfaces if necessary, and then cement them together. Check the alignment from the front, rear, top, and bottom. When the joint is dry, check for any gaps, and sand, fill, and sand again as necessary. If the seams need a lot of work, it helps to mask off the surrounding area so you don't remove any surrounding detail. The wing joint also falls on a natural panel line, so it will have to be restored if it's obliterated.

You can now add the cowl flaps and the horizontal stabilizers. As always, dry-fit the parts first, and when you are satisfied, cement them together. Make sure the stabilizers are also properly aligned by checking them from the front and rear.

Cut the landing gear doors apart, clean them up, and cement them in place. The main gear struts and tail wheel components are painted after the external camouflage finish is applied. In the meantime, they make a nice stand on which to set the model. Just remember they're there, so you don't knock them off.

Painting. Paint your model according to the kit instructions. Before painting,

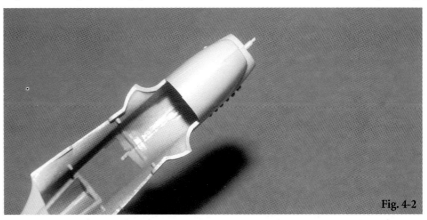

Fig. 4-2

stuff facial tissue into the cockpit and radiator intake as a mask. Airbrush the model with Testor's Model Master Olive Drab FS 34087 on the upper surface, and AeroMaster Neutral Grey on the underside. Thin the olive drab to a 70:30 mix of paint to thinner. The AeroMaster paint is very thin to begin with, so mix it to about 90:10—just enough to keep the paint from building up on the tip of the airbrush. Soft-edge the demarcation between the two colors. You don't need masking, although you can use it to prevent any over spray from getting where you don't want it. If overspray is evident, you can easily touch it up with some thinned paint and a fine brush. Don't forget to spray the drop tank and rack if you're using them.

When the paint is finally dry, add a clear gloss coat in preparation for the decals. We used water-based Microscale Micro Coat and thinned it slightly with water so it would go through the airbrush in a fine mist. The Micro Coat goes on a little differently than the enamel paints, so take a few test shots on some scrap cardboard. Use the cardboard to fine-tune your airbrush settings, pressure, and spraying distance. When you're satisfied with the results, shoot a coat on the model. Let it dry completely. When that paint is dry, you can paint the tail wheel assembly, landing gear struts, and the wheel wells.

Decals. There are only 12 decals to apply, so they go on pretty quickly. Cut the decals apart and apply one at a time according to the kit directions. As a side note: we did not use the red

Fig. 4-3

decal for the fuselage gas cap, since this is painted a flat red later. Apply the decals using warm water and Micro-Set and Micro-Sol decal setting solutions. Dip a decal into the water long enough to completely soak through the backing paper and let it sit for a minute or so until the decal loosens. Then apply a small brush full of Micro-Set to the spot where the decal is to be positioned and place the decal over the solution. Use a soft piece of cotton T-shirt to gently blot out air bubbles from under the decal film and to remove excess water from the model. Next, apply a brush full of Micro-Sol to help the decal snuggle down into the panel lines. Follow this procedure for all the remaining decals. Let the decals dry for 24 hours. Once dry, spray the decals with a fine, even mist of a flat coat, such as Testor's Dullcote Lacquer.

Final assembly. When the Dullcote has dried you can complete the final assembly. Painting and adding the tires, drop tank or bomb, machine guns, propeller and spinner are all that remain (fig. 4-3).

Paint the clear parts by hand with a finely pointed brush, and when dry, add them to the model with Testor's Clear Parts Cement. The cement comes with a fine-tip applicator that lets you place the glue right where you want it. The cement dries clear and does not mar the plastic (much like white glue or Micro Kristal Kleer). If you make a mistake, the glue can be wiped off easily with water.

That's it. Those are the elemental techniques of building a plastic model aircraft out of the box. Learn the basics, and with some practice on small, inexpensive kits, you should have no trouble with other projects.

5

PACIFIC HEAVY METAL

Hasegawa P-40N, 1/72 scale, 49th Fighter Group. Model by Mark Marez

While the Hasegawa P-40N is an old-timer compared to the rest of the items in this review, it's still the best kit compared to competitors such as Matchbox and Monogram. With 36 parts and clear canopy, finely engraved panel lines, nicely done fabric surfaces, and passable small bits, this is the kit to build if you want an accurate N in 1/72 scale. Note this kit, no. AT 103, is the best issue to get.

The "South Pacific Campaign" release provides decals for four different aircraft, two aircraft from the 49th Fighter Group (FG), 7th Fighter Squadron (FS) (including "Rusty"), one aircraft from the 49th FG, 8th FS ("Kay, the Strawberry Blonde") in New Guinea, and one from the 80th FG, 89th FS in India with the massive skull insignia on the nose. The main reason to get this particular kit is that it's in light gray plastic. Past issues of this kit were a dark black-green plastic. Since the aircraft we picked is natural metal with an all white tail and wing leading edges color scheme, the model's plastic

base color of nearly black is not a good idea. Remember, you can't prime natural metal finishes.

The Eduard etched-brass set for the Warhawk also has some important highlights that the well-dressed N shouldn't be without. But by using the True Details resin interior, you can save yourself a lot of work, get a better-looking interior, and come out with some valuable extra parts for your spares box. So don't use the cockpit portions of the Eduard set. Do, however, use most of the wheel and flap well parts on the exterior of the aircraft.

The True Details series of cast-resin interiors for 1/48 and 1/72 scale kits, if you haven't seen them already, are a sight to behold. The set consists of a cockpit base, right and left side walls, control stick, seat, two different instrument panels (one for P-40E-M and one for P-40N) and a gunsight. The amount of detail is excellent. The set also has a complete instruction sheet with FS-595a color data.

Any time you add an aftermarket dress-up kit to a stock model there are always some things that just aren't going to drop right in. While the engineering of aftermarket parts has improved remarkably, some still need a little finagling to make them work. If working both sets into the model seems arduous, keep in mind that Eduard, True Details, and Hasegawa never considered that someone would combine all three into one model. In fact, when this model was first designed and issued, resin and etched-metal detail parts didn't exist.

So, in a nutshell, this project consists of adding the True Details resin cockpit, Eduard photoetched metal wheel wells and flaps, a vacu-formed canopy, a natural metal finish, and scrapbox decals. Not a weekend project by any means.

Cockpit. Now it's time to get to work. Thin out the cockpit side walls on the fuselage halves using no. 16 and no. 10 X-acto blades. Remove the gunsight and the rounded instrument panel

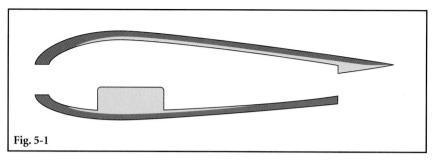

Fig. 5-1

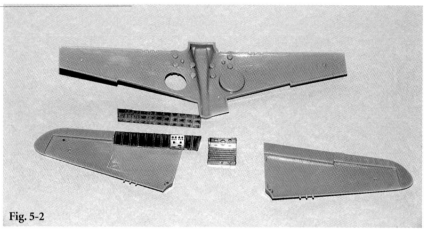

Fig. 5-2

Fuselage. Add more detail to the fuselage using pieces from the Eduard photoetched fret. Form the cowl flaps into a half round shape over a paintbrush handle. Constantly check the curve until it matches the fuselage. When the proper shape has been formed, super glue the assembly to the fuselage. Add the perforated air covers on the upper front of the cowl on top of the engraved kit piece. Then super glue them in place.

Add an aftermarket Squadron vacu-formed canopy no. 9133. Remove the canopy with scissors and an X-acto knife, test-fit it, and sand it to fit the rear section of the cockpit. Set this aside for now. (After the wings and fuselage are permanently attached and the aircraft is polished, attach the rear portion of the canopy with watch-crystal cement and blend it into the fuselage with super glue as a filler.)

Wings. Remove the cast-in wheel wells from the bottom wing half. Try not to cut into the four protrusions alongside of them; these are for the drop tank shackles. Once you've removed the molded-in wheel well cups, continue to remove plastic from the inside wing surface out to the flap-aileron joint using nos. 16 and 10 knife blades. The reason for all this work is that the thick plastic must be removed to make room for the photoetched parts. Remove and fold up the Eduard wheel wells. This will give you an idea of just how deep they are and how much you will need to remove from the inside of the wings to get them to fit. Quite a bit of plastic needs to come from both the top and bottom of the inside wing surfaces. But be careful. If you use a Dremel or other motorized tool, you might melt a hole through the other side. You don't want to have to fix a top wing before shooting a natural metal finish (fig. 5-1).

While you are gutting the wings, there is something you should *not* do. The Eduard instructions show the entire flap that's molded into the upper wings being cut out. Do not do this. The photoetched flaps are supposed to replace the plastic flap molded onto the upper wings. The Eduard instructions tell you to super

shroud area behind it and thin out the underside. Keep an eye also on the cockpit sills and thin those out as well. Check the fit of the resin side walls frequently as you progress. What you are trying to do is make room for the new side walls by removing plastic inside the fuselage halves.

Now on to the interior. While the True Details instruction sheet shows the side walls glued to the cockpit base, it was easier to super glue the right and left side walls to the insides of the fuselage halves. Line up the tops of the side wall sills as far up as they'll go. Sand down the cockpit base quite a bit so it won't interfere with the photoetched wheel wells. Place the base on a piece of 320-grit sandpaper on a flat surface (glass plates are nice).

Using a circular motion, sand a lot of material off. Check the fit of the parts by taping the fuselage halves together and inserting the cockpit base up as far as it will go. Then dry-fit the wings to the fuselage. When the whole assembly fits together with no problems at the wing roots, then you've removed enough from the bottom of the cockpit base.

Now that everything fits together, it's time to paint the interior parts before the fuselage halves are closed up. First spray both the cockpit base and the side walls with Testor's Model Master Interior Green, then accent shadows and recesses with black watercolor. Mix the base color with Testor's Header Flat White and drybrush it over the high points on the base and side walls. On the remaining items in the cockpit (instrument panel, radio boxes, etc.) use a combination of flat black, Classic Black, and Primer Gray. Drybrush this color combination over the blacks as a highlight. Paint the gas tank cover in back of the pilot's seat (under the rear canopy) Interior Green.

After painting the side walls, join the fuselage halves. Be sure you don't forget the front radiator-oil cooler insert. After the fuselage is together, insert the cockpit floor up through the bottom. Super glue it at the corners to hold it in place. Don't glue the instrument panel and gunsight in at this time. They sit high in the cockpit and if inserted make masking off the interior much more difficult. We suggest you add them in the final finishing.

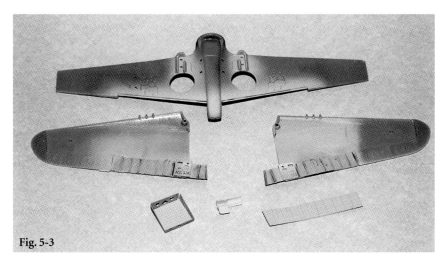

Fig. 5-3

glue a butt joint between two different materials, one noted for bending out of shape. Then they say to try to slide all that together at a wing root joint, fill it, and then polish it out glass smooth so that it can take a metal finish. This would be difficult to achieve so we suggest you deviate from standard assembly procedures.

Here's a better way to deal with the flaps. Remove ¼ the length of the flaps that are on the underside of the bottom wing roots. Using a razor saw is the quickest way. Remove the flaps by scraping them and the surrounding area with your X-acto knife. When you remove the plastic flaps, you'll need to remove quite a bit of plastic from the inside of the wings to let the flaps and wheel well assemblies fit. After a long spell of scraping plastic out of the inside surfaces, start test-fitting the wheel wells and see if you can close the wing halves together. The inside flap wells bend up at a right angle prior to installation. The part that gets bent is supposed to represent the main spar of the wing. It's way too deep to fit into the wing. That part should be cut off using an X-acto knife or a sharp pair of scissors. Same with the small triangle of metal at the end of the flap that you're supposed to bend up to fit into the wing root. It's the wrong shape, so cut it off. Glue a small piece of .010 sheet plastic into the wing root and cut it or sand to the best shape (fig. 5-2).

Gather all of the main plastic parts to the aircraft (fuselage halves,

wings, tail, etc.) and sand them all with a very light grade of sandpaper. Fix any minor flaws from cutting, scraping, and construction errors with super glue and finish final sanding. To install the new brass flaps, super glue the trimmed upper flap onto the area where the old plastic flaps used to be on the underside of the top wing halves. Paint the insides of the wheel well assemblies Interior Yellow. Install wheel wells over the wheel openings in the lower wing half using gel-type super glue. Super glue lengths of wire onto the back edge of the flap wells to act as a ledge to aid placement and gluing of the lower flaps later on (fig. 5-3).

Now you can glue the top and bottom wing halves together. While you're at it, you might as well remove the pitot tube now and drill the wing so you can put it back in during the finishing stage. You might knock it off and lose it if you leave it on. Don't forget to drill out the holes for the gun camera and the landing light on the lower left wing. Now you'll find out whether you've removed enough material from inside the wings so that all the stuff fits. After the wing halves are together, install the flap gusset plates onto the upper flap wells. The instructions show them facing the wrong way. The four small holes on the bottom edge of the plate should face the rear of the aircraft, not in toward the aircraft center.

Drill out the front air inlet in the wing root with a no. 69 drill bit, cut the

kit gun barrels off their housings, and drill the housings with a no. 79 bit. Cut hypodermic tubing to length and add it to the pre-drilled holes. Now join the wings to the fuselage. About the only place there was a fit problem on our model was at the wing root and fuselage joint. We filled this using a gel super glue.

Detail parts. Detail your aircraft wheel struts with brake hoses and more pieces from the photoetched set. You should also use a set of True Details resin wheels no. TD72010. Form the brake hoses from small-diameter wire. Then drill holes into the back side of the resin wheels to attach the hoses. Drill another set of corresponding holes in the front wheel well next to the strut. Form the brake hose and fix it in place with tiny drops of super glue. After the strut assemblies are in place, paint the hoses flat black.

Add only part of the photoetched landing gear door assembly to the aircraft—the forward inside bay of the front landing gear cutout. The other parts don't fit on the kit parts as well, so sand down the plastic doors to reduce their overall thickness.

Painting. Natural metal finishes are probably the most difficult color to paint an aircraft. There are a wide variety of natural metal paint brands, each with its own methods of application and pitfalls to avoid. We chose Testor's Metalizer because of its vast availability and relative ease of application. Make no mistake, all natural metal finishes require much preparation to be successful. Regardless of the product used, the prep work will make or break your finish.

A couple of must-do's with metal finishes are seam preparation and polishing. Fill all the seams with super glue, because it is very hard when it dries. Harder, in fact, than the surrounding plastic when it's fully cured. And it sands glass-smooth. Regular fillers such as hobby putty or automotive fillers leave a porous surface that absorbs the metalizer paint and leaves a grainy texture in the paint. Some putties can be sealed with a coat of super glue afterwards, but why do

Fig. 5-4

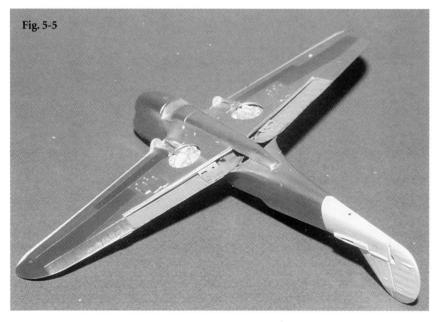

Fig. 5-5

strips of typing paper and dip them into a plate full of water. After letting them soak for a moment, pull the strips out and squeegee them on the edge of the plate. Lay the masks around the panel to be sprayed. You may need to blot them with a paper towel to remove excess water. The surface friction will hold the mask in place while you paint.

An alternative to the wet paper masks is 3M Scotch Removable tape. While it's not as conforming as scotch tape, it is less likely to peel off the Metalizer paint. This tape may leave some adhesive behind so do not leave it on for a long time. Always check the model after you remove tape. If any residue is left, use a piece of fresh tape to clean the surface with a gentle dabbing motion.

Mask various panels and shoot a variety of metalizer colors. We used Stainless Steel-Buffing, Titanium-Buffing, and Aluminum Plate-Buffing mixed with Magnesium-Buffing (as a darking tint) on individual panels as accents. After the metal paints are dry, spray Model Master Classic White on the wing leading edges and tail plane assembly (figs. 5-4 and 5-5).

Spray Pactra Royal Blue on a sheet of clear decal to use for the tail and spinner bands. Use Pactra Bright Blue on the spinner and tail top. The photo caption in Squadron's 49th Fighter Group book says the spinner and tail colors were orange-yellow and blue. However, the illustration on the book cover shows light blue with dark blue stripes. Aircraft using the orange-yellow and blue schemes were from the 8th squadron, not the 7th, which this model represents. Paint the anti-glare panel Aeromaster Black. This is the last color you will spray. Mask it with the wet typing paper so no tape residue gets on the metal finish. Also spray a small square of clear decal film black to use for the canopy framing.

After you finish painting and buffing, spray sealers on the aircraft to protect the paint. We prefer sealers. If you don't use sealers, you must be careful handling the model or you will leave fingerprints. You can try them and see if they work for you. Seal the

everything twice? So, use super glue in the beginning and eliminate a step in finishing the model.

The entire airframe must be polished, so start by sanding the entire surface with 1000-grit sandpaper. This will remove all surface blemishes and prepare the surface for polish. If the surface is relatively free of blemishes (now is the time to be critical) use a 2000-grit paper instead. Now examine the entire surface of the aircraft. If any flaw is visible, sand it out. Polish the model with Blue Magic and cotton T-shirt scraps. Put some polish on the rag and rub in circular motions in small areas until the plastic shines like a freshly waxed and buffed automobile.

After all the parts are polished, wash the model in warm soapy water with a toothbrush to remove the polish residue and let it dry.

Spray the aircraft with Model Master Aluminum Plate-Buffing. Then lightly buff the surface with a clean T-shirt rag. This will make the surface very shiny. This needs to be toned down. Mix 70 percent Aluminum Plate to 30 percent Pactra Metallic Blue and spray it on the model to tone down the surface so the aircraft looks weather-beaten.

After you buff the aircraft, apply different shades of paint to various panels. First make small masks using wet paper. To make these masks, cut

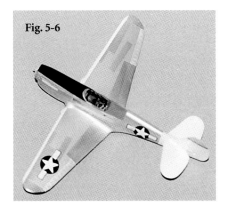

Fig. 5-6

Fig. 5-7

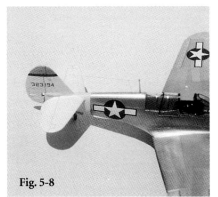

Fig. 5-8

Fig. 5-9

Fig. 5-10

white tail section and leading edges with a flat coat after you apply the decals (fig. 5-6).

Decals. You don't need to put a gloss coat on the aircraft because of the natural metal finish. Piece together decals out of the scrap box. Apply them with Micro-Sol and Micro-Set. We got the serial numbers we put on the rear of our model from a decal sheet of unknown origin. That is a good example of why we don't throw anything away. Our cowl numbers are from a Micro-scale Model railroad sheet (figs. 5-7 and 5-8).

Weathering. Apply washes of black water-based paint to the major control surfaces of the airframe. Wash the white rudder assembly with brown watercolor because the black is too stark. Add fuel stains to the drop tank with the brown wash. Make exhaust stains and gunpowder residue stains with black pastels. Brush them down the fuselage with a no. 1 brush until you achieve the desired effect.

Final assembly. After you attach the landing gear and brake hoses, attach the rest of the photoetched parts, including the struts braces, towing eyelets, and the thinned plastic gear doors.

Apply Bare Metal Aluminum to the canopy framing after you remove the masks. Paint the front wind screen flat black to match the anti-glare panel on the front cowl.

After you paint the drop tank aluminum mount it to the underside of the aircraft. Cut pieces of the etched-brass frame into strips to simulate the sway braces on the side of the tank. Attach them with super glue. Attach the antenna mast and bead sight from the Eduard set on the fuselage last—they are very delicate. Mount the pitot tube in its normal location (fig. 5-9).

Attach an M.V. lens no. 74 to the hole drilled earlier. This represents the landing light on the wing underside. Make an antenna out of stretched sprue and fasten it with super glue to the mast and rudder. Paint it with flat black and use drops of Kristal Kleer to simulate the insulators (fig. 5-10).

6

EXTERIOR COLORS AND MARKINGS

Modelers argue about color more than any other aspect of the hobby. They are often concerned that a color is too green or too brown. While this often leads to some lively discussions at a model club meeting or in the local hobby shop, it seems some paint and decal manufacturers are also getting involved. Well, it's all for the betterment of the hobby and preserving history, as long as people don't get nasty about it.

During WW II, shortages occurred like clockwork. While the military tried to conform to official specifications, officials let nothing hold up the production and delivery of material to the front lines. The hue of paints usually appeared accurate, but sometimes formulas used in mixing them were different. Some paints faded faster and didn't withstand the wear of battle and weather. And harsh climates in Alaska, North Africa, and the Pacific made matters worse. In time, olive drab faded to a variety of greens, browns, or tans. So it was with the P-40.

The XP-40 and the first couple of aircraft were rolled out in natural metal with red, white, and blue rudder stripes, the U.S. star with red center on the upper and lower wings, and "U.S. ARMY" written under the wings.

Service aircraft were quickly painted olive drab and neutral gray with a soft edge and retained the U.S. blue disk, white star, and red spot (known as a cocarde). The insignia was applied to the top and bottom of both wings and eventually appeared on fuselage sides as well. Black wing walks were often applied at the wing root. For a time, the "U.S. ARMY" under the wings was retained, though it was eliminated in mid-1942. Most service

aircraft also had unit and plane-in-unit numbers in black on the tail. The red spot in the U.S. insignia was retained until early 1942. Serial or radio call numbers were added in early- to mid-1942 in yellow across the tail, replacing the earlier unit-plane numbers.

Torch markings (a yellow surround on U.S. insignia) were added to aircraft in the Mediterranean theater from November 1942 through at least mid-1943. The yellow ring appeared on all the insignia or sometimes just fuselage insignia. Many aircraft also carried a U.S. flag on the aft fuselage or vertical tail surfaces. Another flag was often painted on the underside of the wing (usually on the left).

White bars with a red surround were added to the insignia in June 1943. By that time most aircraft were only carrying the wing insignia on the upper left and lower right wings, although there were variations and exceptions. The red surround was deleted in August 1943 and replaced with a blue surround. However, the red surround continued to be placed on some planes for several months after the official change.

During 1942, medium green became popular for its ability to break up the outline of the aircraft. The color was usually applied around the periphery of the horizontal and vertical flying surfaces in the form of scallops, blotches, or continuous waves.

USAAF P-40s operating in the desert were usually painted in an RAF desert scheme of RAF Mid-Stone and Dark Earth over Azure Blue. The patterns were generally identical to those used by the RAF at the time. Later, planes were painted in a U.S. manufactured Sand with Azure Blue, Sky Blue

(lighter than Azure Blue), or Neutral Gray under-surfaces. The Sand color seemed to range from a basic tan to a light pink color. Aircraft painted Sand were seen in the Mediterranean Theater of Operations (MTO) and the South West Pacific Area.

P-40s operated by the RAF were painted in a Dark Earth and Dark Green over Sky scheme with Medium Sea Gray codes and black serials until Summer 1941. Many U.S. P-40s, requisitioned from stocks earmarked for the RAF, were also flown in these camouflage colors and patterns less the codes. After Summer 1941, Dark Green and Ocean Gray over Medium Sea Gray with Sky codes and black serials were used for operations over Europe. RAF P-40s in the desert had the desert scheme described previously.

A Sky-colored spinner and rear fuselage band were added to UK-based aircraft in Spring 1941. Yellow wing leading edges were added in Summer 1941 on U.K.-based aircraft, though not as commonly on MTO aircraft.

British Commonwealth and other nations generally used RAF-style camouflage and markings, conforming to RAF changes as the war progressed. In the Pacific, Australia and New Zealand used P-40s painted in USAAF colors prevalent at the time of delivery—usually Olive Drab over Neutral Gray with and without the Medium Green scalloping on flying surfaces. The Royal Australian Air Force also began using their own mixes of Foliage Green and Light Blue. P-40s delivered to Russia generally started out in an RAF scheme, but later-production aircraft were delivered in the USAAF schemes. The Russians added more camouflage using their own paints.

This Aleutian Tiger is a 1/72 scale P-40E kit from Hasegawa.

The 49th FG natural metal P-40N is also a 1/72 scale Hasegawa.

The P-40B Flying Tiger on this page is a 1/48 scale Monogram kit.

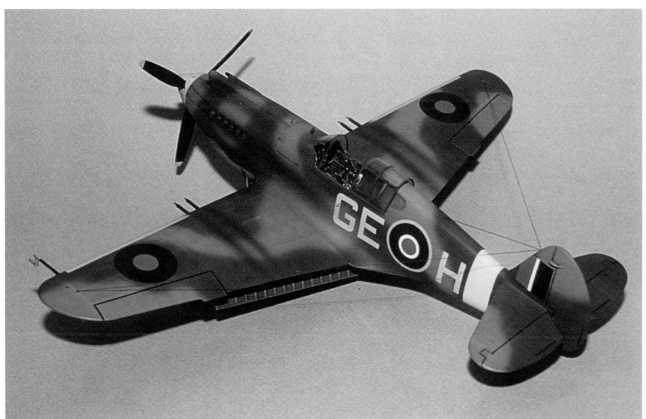

These photos feature the 1/48 scale Monogram P-40B in RAF 26 Sqn colors.

Here and above, Monogram's 1/48 scale Pro Modeler P-40E in Royal Australian Air Force markings.

This page: Mauve's 1/48 scale P-40M kit with P-40F/L conversion parts from Aeromaster in Operation Torch markings.

These photos depict Otaki's P-40K in 1/48 scale in South African markings with parts from Medallion's P-40K conversion kit. The Otaki kit was reissued under Arii and AMT Labels.

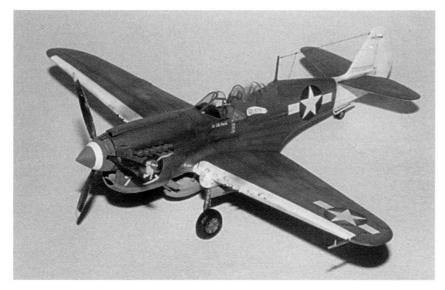

Left and above: Mauve 1/48 scale P-40N in 49th FG markings.

In Desert Pink, ERTL's 1/48 scale P-40N in markings of the 45th FS, 15th FG.

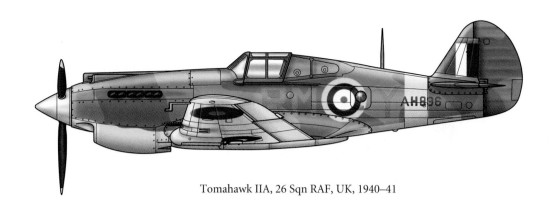

Tomahawk IIA, 26 Sqn RAF, UK, 1940–41

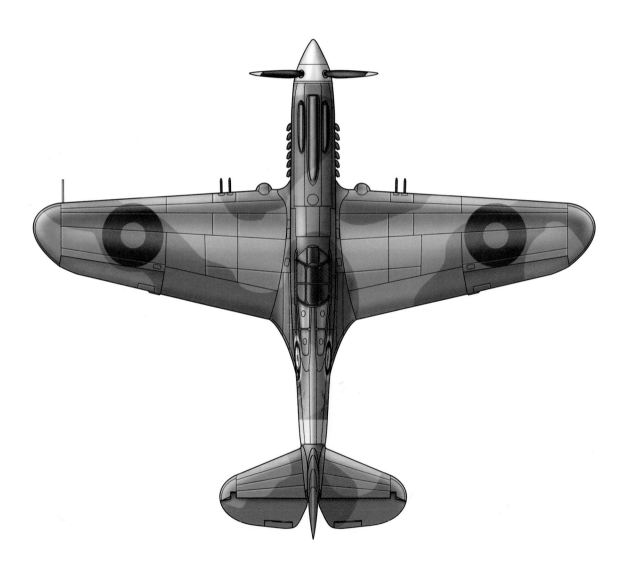

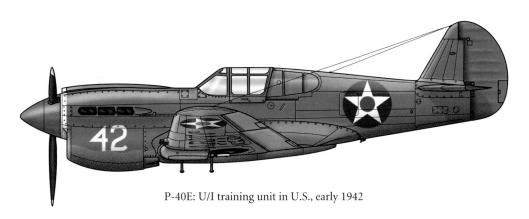

P-40E: U/I training unit in U.S., early 1942

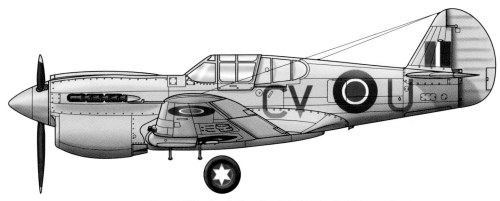

P-40E (Kittyhawk I), 3 Sqn RAAF, North Africa, early 1943

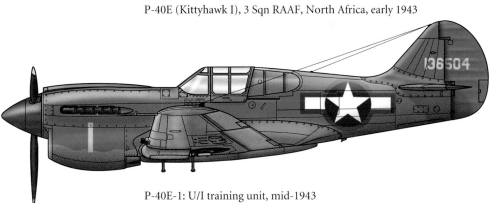

P-40E-1: U/I training unit, mid-1943

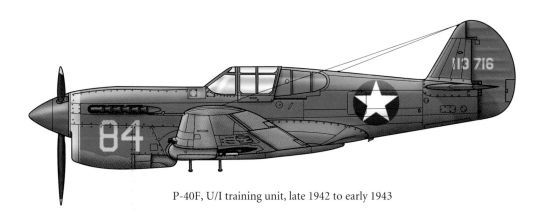

P-40F, U/I training unit, late 1942 to early 1943

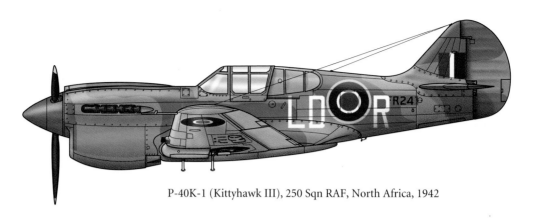

P-40K-1 (Kittyhawk III), 250 Sqn RAF, North Africa, 1942

P-40L, U/I USAAF unit, North Africa, early 1943

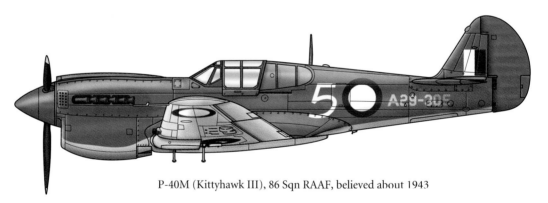

P-40M (Kittyhawk III), 86 Sqn RAAF, believed about 1943

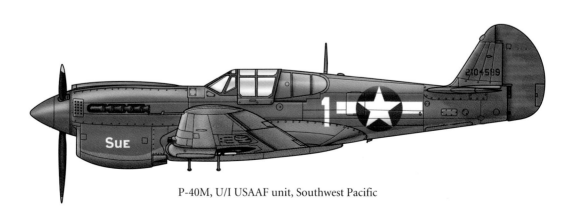

P-40M, U/I USAAF unit, Southwest Pacific

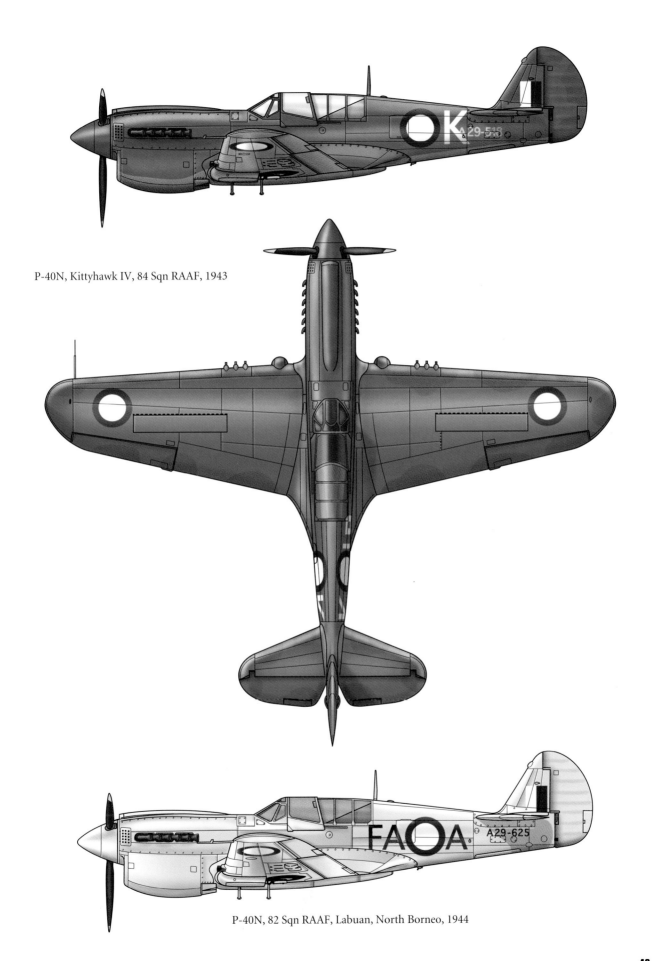

P-40N, Kittyhawk IV, 84 Sqn RAAF, 1943

P-40N, 82 Sqn RAAF, Labuan, North Borneo, 1944

7

NORTHERN EXPOSURE

A P-40E Aleutian Tiger. Model by
Mark Marez

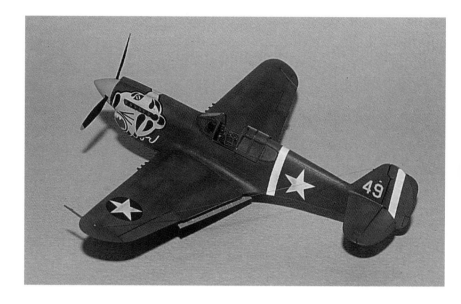

The Hasegawa 1/72 P-40E has been on hobby shop shelves for years. We briefly reviewed the kit in Chapter 4. The kit forms a good base for a moderate detail project since it is basically accurate, but can be improved with the addition of sheet plastic and sprue.

With this kit we will be using "impressionist" modeling to create a visual impression of highly detailed components without replicating every nut, bolt, and rivet. The cockpit will be augmented with additional plastic detailing and the flap area will be removed and detailed by adding dropped flaps and simple sprue detailing. Most of the construction will follow the kit's assembly sequence, deviating slightly where modifications are required.

Cockpit (fig. 7-1). Modify the kit seat by cutting the bottom out of it with a razor saw and thinning the seat side walls with files and sandpaper. Then make a new seat bottom from .010 styrene sheet, using plastic rod on both sides to replicate the seat frame. These additions add a thinner "scale" look.

Remove the kit-supplied gunsight and thin the cockpit side walls with no. 10 and no. 16 X-acto knife blades. Add additional details to the cockpit side walls using strips of .010" plastic, fine wire, and plastic bits from the scrapbox. Reference photos shots will help you place and shape the main items such as armor plates, throttle controls, and auxiliary pump handle. The kit control stick was good enough to keep.

Sand down the kit instrument panel to approximately ⅓ its original thickness. Cut a notch in the upper half of the instrument panel to match the instrument decal. The kit-provided instrument panel and decal are too short and lack the bottom panel. Glue a small piece of sheet plastic to the bottom half of the panel and angle it towards the pilot's seat. Cover the lower instrument panel with a decal from an old P-51 sheet. Finish off the interior with a set of photoetched seat belts from the Eduard P-40N sheet no. 72-131.

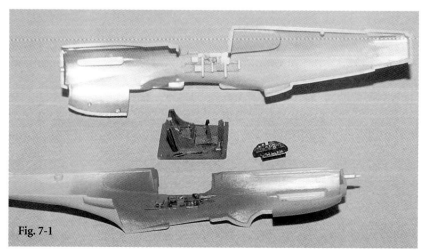

Fig. 7-1

Fig. 7-2

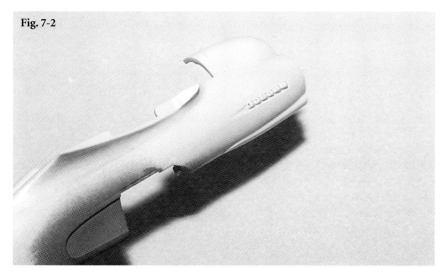

Fig. 7-3

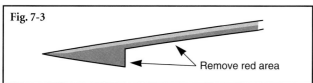

Remove red area

Fig. 7-4

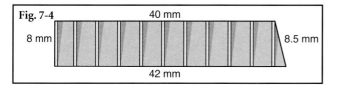

40 mm

8 mm

8.5 mm

42 mm

Make two flaps and reverse one. Note: The written dimensions are for 1/72 scale.

Airbrush the interior, including the area under the two rear windows, using Testor's Model Master Interior Green. Use black watercolor paint to create shadows and add Testor's Header White to the interior green for the drybrush mixture, which you should apply to all the raised detail in the cockpit. Paint major equipment such as radio consoles and electrical panel boxes flat black and drybrush them with Testor's Primer Gray. Enhance and add various switches, knobs, and buttons using super glue or scrap plastic and paint them silver, white, or gray. Drybrush the seat with aluminum paint to replicate the paint chipping found in cockpits in operational aircraft. Paint the photoetched seat belts Tamiya Khaki and the shoulder belts Testor's Classic White. Grind a mixture of tan and brown pastel chalk into the seat belts to give them a dirty appearance.

Fuselage. Assemble the fuselage according to the kit directions except where you add parts or details. Some minor modifications to the fuselage and wing are necessary before it can be assembled. Flatten the exhaust stacks slightly and then drill them out using a .026" drill. Then cement the fuselage together (fig. 7-2).

Wings. This model was supposed to have dropped flaps. Hasegawa sort of complicated things here by molding a portion of the flap on the lower wing half, and the remainder on the upper wing half. Begin by cutting the short length of flap off the underside wing roots. Next grind or scrape away the flap from the bottom of each upper wing half. Be careful not to go too far and break through the upper wing skin (fig. 7-3). Clean the area with an X-acto knife, file, and sandpaper. Make a new set of flaps with .010" sheet styrene. Make the support members for the

inside of the flap with stretched sprue, but don't install the flaps until the finishing stage (fig. 7-4).

Modify the gun barrels by carefully drilling them out using a .020" drill bit. Then cement the wings to the fuselage. This kit needed very little filling despite its age. A slight gap appeared along the lift wing root which we filled with white glue. The joint between the chin scoop and the bottom wing assembly also had a slight step, which we easily cured with a spot of putty. Construct the rest of the kit according to the instructions.

Painting. Paint and mark the model according to the AeroMaster decal sheet 72-022, Fighting Warhawks. Spray the fuselage and tail bands, located behind the rear cockpit windows and on the rudder, with Testor's Classic White. Since the paint is a gloss you will have to wait 48 hours for the paint to dry before masking. You can use Bare Metal Foil to mask the bands. Then, apply Testor's Gray Primer to the entire aircraft. Check and touch up all joints, seams, etc. as needed. We mixed Testor's Zinc Chromate Green and Insignia Yellow to make the interior yellow color. You can use this color along with Zinc Chromate Green as an anti-corrosion paint in weapons' bays, flap and wheel wells, and engine compartments. You can also paint the model's wheel wells, inside the flaps, landing gear wells, and covers this color. Use white glue to set the landing gear doors and tail wheel doors in place after spraying the wheel wells Interior Yellow, but before spraying the bottom color Neutral Gray. That way they serve as a mask to cover the wheel wells.

After masking off the flap wells and wheel wells, paint the entire lower portion of the aircraft with neutral gray. (Don't forget to spray the other half of the flaps.) When that's dry, mask off the cockpit and rear window cutouts. Use scotch tape to mask off the demarcation line on the rear fuselage between the top and bottom colors. Cut out a piece of card stock to use on the nose area. Simply turn the mask over from one side to another. When

Fig. 7-5

all the masking is in place, spray Aero-Master's Olive Drab as the top color.

You can lighten the standard neutral gray with a few drops of white and spray it on the fabric surfaces on the underside of the aircraft elevators and ailerons. You can also use this color to accent the major panel lines of the model's underside. To weather the top side of the aircraft, begin by spraying a light coat of AeroMaster's Faded Olive Drab. Dust this on the very top of the fuselage surfaces, spine, forward edge of tail, top of the engine cowling and scoop, and the very forward edge of the wings all the way to the wing tips. Also spray this color on the upper fabric surfaces of the rudder, ailerons, and elevators (fig. 7-5).

Create the faded paint effect by first using a 70:30 thinner and paint mixture of AeroMaster airbrush thinner and Faded Olive Drab paint. Spray a small area inside an area framed by panel lines with the mixture. Do this throughout the upper wing surfaces and rudder assembly. This process has to be done gradually, because you don't want the transitions to be harsh. Keep making passes over the area until you have almost achieved the desired effect, then stop. Remember, don't create too much contrast in this area.

Finally, spray the spinner insignia yellow and the prop blades flat black with yellow tips. When the paint dries, apply a gloss coat in preparation for the decals.

Decals. We used Aeromaster's P-40 sheet no. 72-022 Fighting Warhawks E's and K's . Apply your decals using Micro-Sol and Solvaset setting solutions. Use Solvaset cut down with lots of water only in the most difficult situations, because it sometimes leaves a white residue embedded in the decal when used right out of the bottle. Apply the Aleutian Tiger head decals one at a time on either side of the engine cowling. Before removing the left side tiger head decal from the sheet, cut a line in the decal so you can install it over the exhaust stacks. Using a sharp X-acto blade, cut a line in the decal sheet slightly longer than the exhaust stacks. The cut will start just below the eye and run from the nostril back to the ear.

After wetting the decal and removing it from the backing, brush it with some Micro-Sol and position it. Place the cut over the stacks and, with a soft brush wetted with Micro-Sol, work as much of the solution into the area as possible, and position the decal. Making a very small cut at the spinner (intake junction right below the nostril) on the decal will help it sit down on that curved spot. The exhaust stacks should protrude through the decal at this point. Leave the decal to dry. When nearly dry, the decal should draw down onto the stacks and over and into the lip of the radiator inlet (under the spinner). Again, using a sharp X-acto blade, a tweezers, and a straight edge, carefully cut away the decal hanging onto the stacks. Work slowly. If your cuts are not sharp and clean, the decal will crack when you try to remove it.

When you have removed as much of the decal as is needed to uncover the exhausts, rewet the area to help the remaining decal snuggle down over the opening. Re-apply the setting solution as needed to get the decal to sit all the way down. Use a soft brush wetted with Micro-Sol on the mouth (red) area to get the decal to wrap into the radiator intake. Gently brush the edge of the decal into the intake and let it dry. You may need to do this a number of times before it finally lies down.

After the decal is down on one side, check the alignment. The top of the decal (the ear) should touch the centerline of the aircraft on the cowl air scoop. The bottom edge of the decal should line up with the model centerline along the radiator inlet bottom where the fuselage halves are split.

This is important when using wraparound style markings like this. Getting both ends to meet and everything to line up in the middle can be difficult. Many decals of this type, particularly on engine cowlings where there are compound curves, are printed too short, and their ends don't meet when installed (fig. 7-6).

In the case of AeroMaster's tiger head, the right side is too long. Follow the same procedure as previously outlined with a few exceptions. The top part of the right side decal (top ear) fits flush and connects to the installed decal. Both have a flat edge at the top of the ears where they come together along the top of the air scoop. Remove 3/32" from the bottom of the decal where the tiger's mouth is. Then the right side decal should fit down with little or no overlap along the radiator bottom. After the decals are set, spray the model with Micro Flat.

Weathering. You completed the first part of the weathering earlier with the paint fading. Do some additional weathering by using black and dark brown pastel chalks. Scrub small amounts of ground-up chalk into selected panel lines. Blow or wipe away the excess chalk. You can create exhaust, gunpowder burns, and dirt marks by rubbing small amounts of ground-up chalk into the area behind the outlet and streaking it back in a straight line.

Apply black watercolor to all the major recessed lines on the aircraft (rudder hinge line, ailerons, elevators, gun gas ports, and shell ejection chutes). This adds depth and breaks up the monotony of the large areas of olive drab paint. Apply the wash to both the top and bottom of the aircraft. After letting it dry thoroughly, spray the model with several light coats of Testor's Dullcote (fig. 7-7).

Final finishing. Detail the landing gear with small-diameter wire brake hoses. Drill holes in the brake hubs using the photos as a guide. Super glue the wires into the holes and form it around the strut. Drill corresponding holes into the upper wheel well to insert the rest of the brake tubing (fig. 7-8).

Fig. 7-6

Fig. 7-8

Use a Squadron vacu-formed canopy instead of the kit canopy. The rear see-though windows (not provided with the Squadron canopy) are from the kit. Polish them with Blue Magic plastic polish and install them with Micro Kristal Kleer. Cover a small square of clear decal sheet with faded olive drab paint to make into frames for the canopy. Cut the decal into strips and lay them over the canopy framing and snuggled them down with Micro-Sol. Attach the canopies using Hypo-tube (watch-crystal cement). Flatten the kit tires by holding them against a hot iron, then scrape and file them clean. Take a new 75-gallon drop tank from the latest issue 1/72 scale Hasegawa P-51D kit to replace the old one provided in the kit. Fashion support struts for the tank from scrap wire and white glue them into place. Make antenna lines from stretched clear sprue and attach them with Germanow-Simpson Hypo-Tube watch crystal cement (available from Micro-Mark Tools) (fig. 7-9).

Fig. 7-7

Exhaust and gun streaks

Black watercolor added

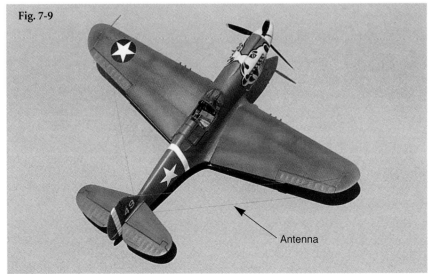

Fig. 7-9

Antenna

8

THE FLYING TIGERS

A little something extra for Monogram's P-40B. Model by Tom Neely

The Monogram P-40B has been around for longer than many of us care to remember, dating back to the mid-1960s. The kit featured a little more than 60 parts, finely raised panel lines and rivets, cockpit detailing (both molded on and added), an open or closed canopy option, and separate flaps that could be positioned open or closed. Though not without fault, this was a very fine kit at the time. If it had been a bit better, this kit could have

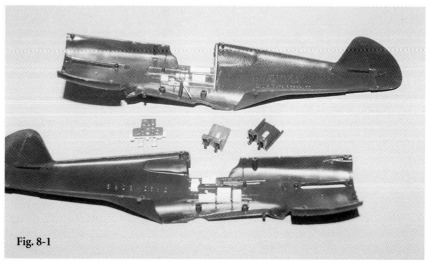

Fig. 8-1

Fig. 8-2

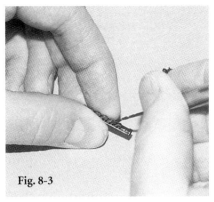
Fig. 8-3

been a prime candidate for inclusion in Monogram's Pro-Modeler series. The kit has been reissued a number of times over the years and the aftermarket decal manufacturers have kept pace, issuing several decal sheets covering U.S., British Commonwealth, and other modelers. Since this book would be incomplete without at least one Flying Tiger project, it seemed only natural that we use this kit as the example.

Consistent with the theme of this book, we customized this kit until it was well beyond what Monogram intended the finished model to be. We did the usual drilling, thinning, and shaving of parts, but also added a new interior, brake lines, wheel well liners, and some rescribed panel lines.

Cockpit (fig. 8-1). You will begin by scratchbuilding much of the interior, although you will use some kit-supplied interior parts after you modify them a bit. First, and using reference photos as a guide, you can spruce up the cockpit side walls and their kit parts (9 and 10) using .010" sheet plastic, stretched sprue, and copper wire to make new panels, boxes, a map case, control rods and lever, etc. Make knobs on the levers from small drops of super glue and the oxygen hose from fine copper electrical wire tightly wound around a piece of .030" to .040" stretched sprue. Hold the ends of the wire in place with a drop of super glue. The wire gives the sprue some rigidity and enables you to bend it in almost any shape you want. Paint most of the interior Model Master Interior Green. Paint electrical boxes and other small details flat black and drybrush them with a dark gray. Paint the oxygen hoses olive drab and drybrush them with light gray.

Modify the kit seat by first filling the kit pilot's mounting slot in the backrest. Remove the framework on the back of the seat. Cement a piece of .010" sheet plastic to the front of the seat to replicate the cupped front end of the seat bucket. Paint the seat Floquil Old Silver and the molded seat cushion AeroMaster Faded Olive Drab. Make lap and shoulder harnesses from masking tape, cut them to size, and paint them Model Master Camouflage Gray. Make hash marks down the center of the belts with a drafting pencil after the paint is dry. Cut the belt buckles out of tiny lengths of Fineline drafting tape and super glue them into position. Paint the buckles Model Master Chrome Silver. Assemble all of these off the seat. When the everything is dry, attach them to the seat using super glue. Attach the seat to the kit floor.

The kit-supplied instrument panel is completely wrong for this aircraft. P-40s mounting the nose guns had an upside-down T-shaped instrument panel. The breech end of the guns were visible along the sides of the T where they could be manually charged by the pilot.

Make a new panel by combining two panels of .010" and .015" sheet plastic cut to the proper shape. Punch out the locations of the instruments in the .010" sheet with a Waldron Punch-and-Die set. If you don't have this set, use a small circle-drawing template to find the center point of each instrument. Using a sharp pencil, draw a light line around the perimeter of each circle as a guide. Use appropriate-sized drill bits to drill out the instruments. Once the holes are made, sandwich the two sheets together and mark the instruments' locations on the back sheet. Fashion an instrument bezel for the center of the panel using .010" sheet plastic with a hole the same size as the instrument. Then carefully cut the plastic into a square shape and cement it to the outer panel. Add other small details to the outer panel with sub-miniature discs cut out with the Waldron punch.

Place the instrument decals from the spares box (or the store) over the previously marked location. It's important to continually check the location of the decals with the outer panel while you're adding them in case they float out of position. Take your time.

After the decals are dry, paint the outer panel AeroMaster Tire Black. Then carefully cement the two panels together, again making sure the instrument faces line up with their respective holes. Then give the panel a light dry-brushing with Model Master Neutral Gray. Put a good-size drop of Micro Kristal Kleer onto the face of each instrument to replicate the glass faces.

Using the width of the kit instrument panel as a guide, cut a length of small Plastruct I-beam to length. Center the new instrument panel on the I-beam and cement the two together. Next, cut a small piece of .010" sheet plastic the same length as the I-beam and 3/32" wide and cement this, with a slight upward tilt, to the bottom edge of the instrument panel. These parts represent the span-wise bracket that supported the instrument panel. Add some sheet-plastic discs for knobs and dials and stretched sprue for the gun charging handles. Paint the assembly interior green and dry-brush it with neutral gray. Make the knobs and handles tire black, red, and neutral gray.

Make new rudder pedals using .015" plastic rod for the arms and .010" plastic sheet for the pedals. Cut them to shape, glue them together, and cement them to the back of the instrument panel. Paint them interior green and drybrush them with neutral gray and a touch of Floquil Old Silver in the high-wear area of the pedals.

Fashion a new rear bulkhead from sheet plastic and add lightening holes with the punch set. Paint the bulkhead interior green and cement it in place behind the seat (fig. 8-2).

Fuselage. Begin the fuselage assembly by cleaning the mold seams off the exhausts and drilling out their ends (fig. 8-3). Then cement the exhausts into place and install the cockpit interior components. Cement the fuselage halves together, and fill their seams with super glue and rub them down with 400- and 600-grit wet or dry sandpaper. When complete, you can attach the nose after first making a choice. If you want the prop to spin, add the prop shaft and rear spinner. If you want the prop cemented in place, or you want it removable, then cement the prop shaft in place before attaching the nose to the fuselage. Remove the seams as previously described, but note the seam around the lip of the radiator intake falls on a natural panel line which must be restored if it's damaged. Leave the cowl flaps in the closed position. You will need to rescribe the center flap separation line.

Rescribe all of the major panel lines with a Bare Metal Foil Scribing Tool. Then drill out all of the Dzus fasteners on the engine cowlings with a no. 78 (.0225) drill bit. Don't drill all the way through the plastic—just enough to make a noticeable recess for a black wash. Also, drill out the machine gun barrels on the top of the cowling. Finally, add a small piece of stretched sprue to the vertical tail to replicate the rudder horn (fig. 8-4).

Wings. The only modifications you need to make to the wings are to drill out the shell ejection ports and the landing light and add canvas wheel well liners and a plastic plug to the wheel strut openings in the bottom of the wing. Back the shell ports and the hole for the landing light with .010" sheet plastic (fig. 8-5).

When retracted, the landing gear struts are actually outside the wing surface. The wing surface forms the roof for the strut well. Monogram left a hole in this area, which lets you see inside the wing. Block this off with a piece of .010" sheet plastic cut to shape (fig. 8-6) and cement it in place. Cement the kit

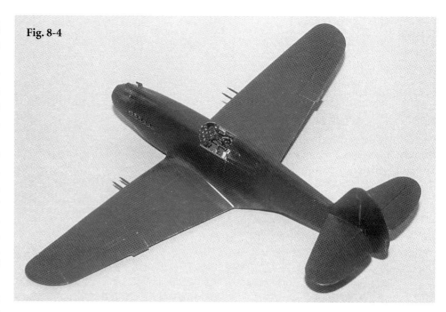

Fig. 8-4

Fig. 8-5

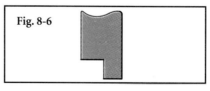

Fig. 8-6

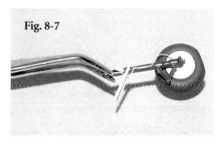

Fig. 8-7

flaps in the closed position after first removing their pivots and the small tabs that hold them closed.

Some P-40s carried liners in their wheel wells to keep foreign matter out of the inside of the wing. Add the liners to this model using thin metal foil. In this case, we used the foil wrappers from some See's chocolate candies. Of course, we had to eat the chocolates so they wouldn't go to waste. Gently push

the foil wrappers into place until they line the well up to the wing surface. Use a fine bead of super glue to anchor the foil in place. Go easy here and try not to get glue on the outer surface of the wing. Once the glue dries (a couple of minutes), trim off the excess foil with a sharp hobby knife blade.

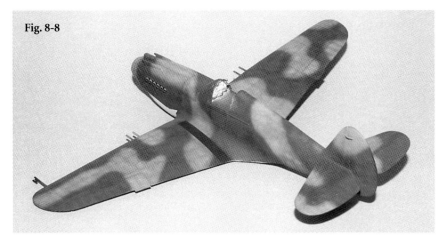

Fig. 8-8

Fig. 8-9

cement. When the glue is dry and the windscreen securely locked in place, carefully brush a bead of thinned Kristal Kleer into the seam to fill any gaps. Then mask off the inner portion of the windscreen, canopy, and cockpit in preparation for painting.

Add the tail wheel well and doors (part 20) to the aft fuselage. Make small door retraction struts from copper wire and super glue them in place.

Painting (fig. 8-8). First, give the model a light primer coat to help you detect any flaws in the seams. Repair any flaws and then spray interior green onto the windscreen and canopy. Next, paint the undersides type S Floquil British Sky. After the paint is dry, mask off the undersurfaces of the horizontal stabilizers and fuselage sides and spray the upper surface with Floquil British Dark Earth. Then spray on Floquil British Dark Green, using the pattern supplied with the AeroMaster decal sheet. Then lighten the Dark Earth and Dark Green a bit and respray it onto the surface to fade the individual panels (fig. 8-9). Mask off the wing walkways and paint them tire black. Also use tire black to paint the radiator intake area under and behind the spinner. When all the paint is dry, remove the fuselage and tail plane masks and give the airframe a coat of Microscale Micro Gloss in preparation for the decals.

Decals. We used AeroMaster decal sheet 48-056, Foreign Tomahawk Collection, on our project. Apply your decals with a setting and solvent solution. Spray a fine coat of thinned light gray paint onto the decals to tone them down so they match the look of the camouflage paint.

Weathering. Use thinned artist's oil paint as a wash to deepen the shadows in the engraved cowl panels, control surfaces, landing gear details, etc. Spray a coat of Testor's Dullcote onto the model to seal the decals, oils, and to give the model the proper flat sheen. Use thinned tire black to replicate exhaust and gunpowder streaks on the fuselage and wings (fig. 8-10).

Certain areas of the wing and tailplane leading edges and areas along the wings and cowling are normally

Smooth away excessive wrinkling with a pencil eraser or something similarly soft. If you tear the foil, use thinned white glue or Micro Kristal Kleer to fill the hole.

Cement the wings to the fuselage without further ado. If the fit isn't good do some dry-fitting, trimming, and more dry-fitting where necessary to ensure tight wing root seams and a proper dihedral. Use a thin plastic strip as a shim to fill any gaps if necessary. Take the time to get it right. Finally, fill in the mounting hole for the belly tank.

Detail parts. Use the kit landing gear struts after you cut off the single retraction strut and clean off the mold parting lines. Make a pair of new retraction struts for each leg using a

.015" square plastic strip. Cement a tiny disc of .010 sheet plastic to the joint where the struts meet the leg to represent the hinge point. A thin slice of plastic rod will work just as well. Cement all in place but don't paint them until after you apply the external camouflage finish and decals (fig. 8-7).

Use a Squadron vacu-formed canopy and windscreen in lieu of the kit-supplied clear parts. Use the kit's rear quarter lights since their fit is pretty good, but don't add them until after you paint and add decals. Carefully cut out the new windscreen with sharp scissors and a fairly new hobby knife blade. First mask off the windscreen and canopy with 3M Frosted Transparent Tape. Then attach the windscreen to the fuselage with liquid

Fig. 8-10

Fig. 8-12

Fig. 8-11

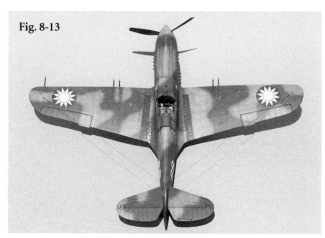

Fig. 8-13

subject to prop blast or maintenance wear and tear. To create this affect, use a toothpick to dab on a few small touches of silver paint (fig. 8-11). Also apply a thin misty coat of tan or light brown along areas of wear on the tires and on the upper surfaces of the model to simulate the accumulation of dust and dirt. Remember, the Flying Tigers did not have the luxury of hard surface runways and usually flew from dirt or grass fields. Make sure the paint comes out as a fine mist and doesn't spatter on the surface of the model. Use a high pressure setting on your compressor and make quick passes stopping and starting each spray away from the model (fig. 8-12).

Final assembly. In the final assembly you should remove the canopy masks, attach the landing gear and stretched sprue brake lines, paint the landing light bright silver and fill it in with Kristal Kleer, paint the gun barrels Testor's Gun Metal and drybrush them with neutral gray, and add a set of Teknics no. TK7207 photoetched metal gun sights. Lastly, add fine nylon sewing thread, painted black, to replicate the antenna wires (fig. 8-13).

9
A YANK IN THE RAF

Model by Tom Neely

Now that you've got your feet wet building the P-40B, this project will take you further by adding the True Details etched-brass interior set with additional scratchbuilt details, scratchbuilt flap wells, new cowl flaps, wheels, a vacu-formed canopy, and the drop tank and its associated plumbing.

Preparing the conversion parts. You will need two things when working with photoetched metal parts: a sharp pair of fine-pointed scissors, shears, or a hobby knife; and super glue. Most photoetched parts are attached to a fret (metal sprue). Remove them and clean off any burrs. A pair of sharp scissors is probably the best tool for 90 percent of this work. Use super glue to attach the parts to the model, whether it's plastic, resin, or metal.

Cockpit. Use the True Details cockpit set according to the set's instructions

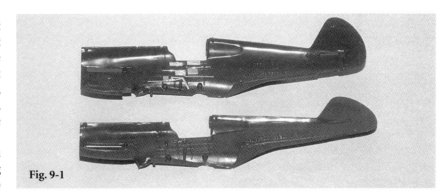

Fig. 9-1

and various reference photos, such as those in this book and *P-40 Warhawk in Action* by Squadron/Signal Publications. Attach the parts with super glue. Make additional details using thin strands of copper wire, discs of .010" and .015" plastic you can cut out with a Waldron Punch and Die Set (or thin wafers of plastic rod of various diameters) to replicate knobs, buttons,

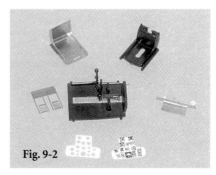

Fig. 9-2

switches, etc. Use plastic rod for the interior map lights on the cockpit sides. Use flattened stretched sprue to make the cowl flap actuator. Glue it to small, crescent-shaped pieces of .010" and .015" plastic sheet. Make an oxygen hose from fine copper wire wrapped around a length of stretched sprue using super glue to anchor the ends of the wire. Enhance some of the lever knobs and handles with a small drop of super glue to create a three-dimensional look and to make the parts stand out better. Photoetched parts are basically a two-dimensional medium. They have length and width, but lack depth. Certain things, such as a tubular control stick, can't be effectively rendered with etched metal. Because of this, some parts on photoetched frets are not usable. Keep this in mind, since there are times when sprue or rod are going to do a better job (fig. 9-1).

Make the cockpit bulkhead behind the seat (see Chapter 8, fig. 8-2) from .010" sheet plastic with .035" lightening holes punched along the edges. Glue the bulkhead into place using the kit floor and seat as a guide if necessary. Fold up the True Details seat and add the seat adjustment and seat belt tensioning levers on both sides of the seat pan. Make these from small pieces of sprue with super glue knobs. Also make the adjustment rail and cross brace behind the seat from small lengths of stretched sprue.

Assemble the kit floorboard (in this case, the top surface of the wing) according to the kit and True Details instructions. Remove the foot pads at the front. Add a small hydraulic line off the back of the hydraulic pump on the right side of the cockpit floor (fig. 9-2).

After all the cockpit details are complete, airbrush the entire area except the seat and instrument panel with Testor's Model Master Interior Green. Paint some panels and boxes on the side, the throttle quadrant, and other minor details AeroMaster Tire Black. Pick out details in flat red and medium gray. Paint the instrument panel tire black with the instrument faces picked out in Model Master

Fig. 9-3

Camouflage Gray. Paint the oxygen hose Model Master Olive Drab and drybrush it with a light shade of gray and weather it with oils. Airbrush the seat with Floquil Old Silver. Then drybrush the entire cockpit, except the seat, with Model Master Neutral Gray to bring out the highlights and give everything a faded and worn look.

Then give the cockpit a clear gloss coat. Let this dry for 24 hours before applying a wash to deepen the shadows. Create a mixture of Grumbacher black and burnt sienna oil paint and thin it with several drops of Turpenoid. Wash the entire interior with this mixture and drybrush selected areas, mainly high spots, with neutral gray. Paint the canvas portion of the seat belts camouflage gray and the leather portions AeroMaster Japanese Red-Brown. Paint the buckles Model Master Chrome Silver. Once painted, form-fit them over the seat and super glue them in place. Then super glue the seat to the cockpit floor (fig. 9-3).

Fuselage. Display the cowl flaps in the open position. First, carefully remove the kit flaps from the fuselage shells. Set these aside for later. Make a plug for the cowl flap well from .010" sheet plastic (see template, fig. 9-4). Cement this plug in place approximately ⅜" ahead of the cowl flap hinging point and paint it flat black. It's suppose to block the view into the interior of the bare fuselage.

Fig. 9-4

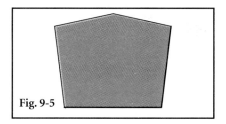

Fig. 9-5

Dress up the kit exhausts by first cleaning the mold seam lines and running a file across the end of each pipe to flatten them. Drill out the ends with a .055" drill bit or a new no. 11 X-acto (or equivalent) blade. It will help considerably if you have pilot holes made with a pin or small drill bit. Cement the exhausts into the fuselage shells.

Glue the completed seat and floor assembly into the cockpit per the kit instructions. Glue the instrument panel to the small molded-in tabs protruding from the front portion of each side wall, then glue both fuselage halves together. Fill the seams with super glue. Try not to remove too much of the raised panel line and rivet detail when sanding the seams down. After sanding the seams to your satisfaction, attach the nose and spinner sub-assembly to the fuselage front. Dry-fitting and trimming are needed to get a good fit.

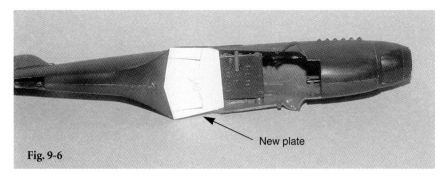

Fig. 9-6

New plate

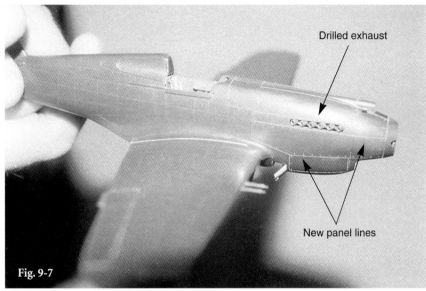

Fig. 9-7

Drilled exhaust

New panel lines

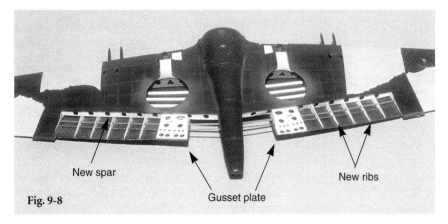

Fig. 9-8

New spar

Gusset plate

New ribs

Wings. Now prepare the wings for assembly and the scratchbuilt flap well detail. Start by cutting out the holes for the shell ejection ports in the bottom of the wing. Next, drill out the landing light to the diameter of an M.V. Products lens no. LS-11 (.199"), but don't glue in the lens until the final assembly phase after painting and decaling. Cut a .010" sheet plastic plug (see template in Chapter 8, fig. 8-6) for the landing gear strut well. This represents the exposed portion of the wing inside the landing gear pod. Finally, use 400- and 600-grit sandpaper to smooth out the exposed area of the flap wells on the inside of the upper wing halves. Also, sand down the adjacent areas of the wheel well openings to prepare them for detailing later.

To detail the flap wells, cut four strips (two for each wing) of .010" sheet plastic, 3/32" wide by 2³⁄8" long. These will form the front edge of the wing flap well and the rear portion of the main wheel box. Punch or drill a series of .081" lightening holes about ¼" apart along the centerline length of the strips. Use the reference photos as a guide. Next, glue one strip along each side (front and rear) of the raised plastic rib or spar at the front of the flap well on the lower wing half.

Make 20 (10 per wing) .010" sheet plastic wedges, 3/32" deep at the base, ½" long and narrowing to a point. Four of these will box in the ends of the flap wells while the remaining 16 will be used replicate the ribs inside the flap wells. Glue one wedge in each end of each flap well on the upper wing half, making sure to butt the wide end up against the strip at the front of the flap well. Space the remaining eight wedges (about ¼") within the well and glue them in place.

Now for the fun part. When the wedges are set hard, use a straightedge and make two marks about ⅛" apart along the top of each of the wedges and running in a line along the span of the wing. Using the marks and reference photos as a guide, drill a pair of holes in each wing. Use a no. 66 drill bit for the front holes and a no. 76 bit for the rear holes. Next, run a 2³⁄4" length of

Finally, since this project has new dropped flaps, make a .010" plug for the lower aft fuselage to block the view into the fuselage. The plug (see template, fig. 9-5) represents the exposed portion of the wing flap opening on the top half of the wing. Carefully dry-fit the plug before cementing it in place along the lower edge of the fuselage bottom under the cockpit. The rear portion of this plug, when properly fitted, will look like the inner surface of

the upper wing halves and will blend right into the fuselage and wing trailing edge joint (fig. 9-6).

When all the seams are filled, rescribe all the cowling panel lines. Use ⅛" and ¼" Fineline tape as a guide for your scriber. Use a no. 78 drill bit to remove the Dzus fasteners on the cowl panels as well. Just drill deep enough to make a shallow impression. Also, drill out the nose guns with a no. 75 bit (fig. 9-7).

.030" diameter rod into the front row of holes for the flap actuator and the same length of .020 rod through the rear row of holes for the aileron actuator (fig. 9-8).

Next, cut out the wing gusset plate from .010" sheet plastic and add the lightening holes with a drill or punch set (see template). Some of the holes are oval, so you must elongate them with a round file. Glue the gusset plate in place between the second and third rib (from the fuselage outward). Paint the flap wells interior green, give them an oil-paint wash, and drybrush them with neutral gray.

Use the kit flaps, but you will have to remove some sink marks and ejection marks prior to painting. Paint and weather the flaps as described previously, but don't add them until the final assembly phase.

Tackle the wheel wells next. Completely box in the wheel well with strips of .010" sheet plastic approximately ³/₈" wide. Detail the inner faces of the side ribs with thin sheet plastic and add three lightening holes to the front spar. Note the middle hole is triangular. Use the reference photos as a guide. Glue these parts to the lower wing section about 2 mm from the edge of the wheel opening. Next, glue several .015" (or smaller) square strip stringers onto the inner surface of the upper wing. You can add hydraulic lines snaking through the holes in the front spar with copper wire bent to shape and secured with super glue. Paint the wheel wells as you did the flap wells (figs. 9-9 and 9-10).

Now add the wings to the fuselage. If you find, as we did, that the fit of the wing root is poor, use .010" sheet plastic as a shim to eliminate large gaps. Fill smaller gaps with super glue. Make sure the proper dihedral is present, since the wings tend to look a little flat. When the seams are finished off, fill in and smooth the hole for the belly tank and drill in the cockpit vent hole in the leading edge of the right wing root fairing.

Detail parts. Cut out the four individual cowl flaps from .010" sheet plastic and make copies of the kit flaps re-

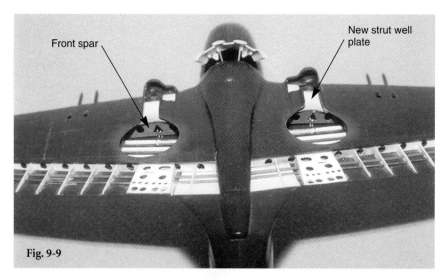

Fig. 9-9

Front spar

New strut well plate

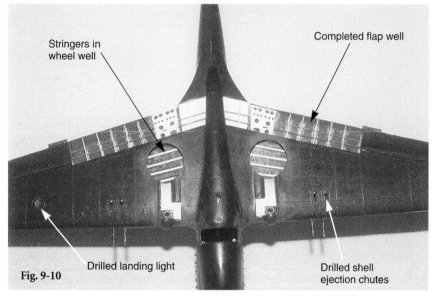

Fig. 9-10

Stringers in wheel well

Completed flap well

Drilled landing light

Drilled shell ejection chutes

moved earlier from the fuselage shells. The major difference is that the new individual flaps are tapered, being about ¹/₃₂" wider at one end than the other. They are also thinner and more to scale. Slightly bend each flap so it follows the curvature of the fuselage. Next, glue the wide end of the cowl flap to the fuselage starting at one end and work your way around to the other with the flaps barely touching each other. Position them open at about a 30- to 40-degree angle. After the glue has thoroughly dried, cut out small triangular shaped .010" thick pieces of plastic to fill in the gaps between the flaps. Attach the narrow end to the cowl in this case.

Now add flap actuator rods with fine copper wire, stretched sprue, sheet plastic, and .015" rod. If the fit is tight and there isn't a lot of working room, take your time and use one or more pairs of tweezers.

Paint and weather the interior of the flaps as you did the wing flaps, just be careful when you drybrush them. You don't want to knock anything off (fig. 9-11).

Also detail the belly tank and mount. Cement the belly tank together and, when dry, remove the seams. Clip off the round peg on top of the tank. Make a new tank pylon by laminating together two pieces of .015" strip that are ⁵/₁₆" long. After cutting, filing, and shaping the pylon, drill a small .030" (no. 66 bit) hole in each end of the bracket. Glue the bracket to the fuselage centerline.

Tank pylon and sway braces

Cowl flaps

Fig. 9-11

Fig. 9-12

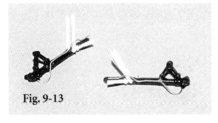

Fig. 9-13

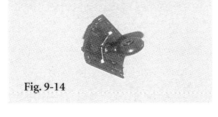

Fig. 9-14

rod will work just as well. Glue the cross supports in place with super glue. Glue a small .010" disc to the ends of the braces at an angle that matches the curvature of the tank. Frequently test-fit.

Finally, add a fuel line from the tank to the fuselage with fine copper wire. Use the wire to represent the rigid piping. Use a small sleeve of sprue slipped over the wire to represent the flexible rubber hose that is part of the fuel line. Or use telephone wire with the insulation stripped off the ends. Bend it to shape and insert it into holes drilled in the fuselage and the tank. Paint the fuel line, tank, and support assemblies the same color as the bottom of the fuselage, and paint the flexible portion of the fuel line tire black (fig. 9-12).

Prepare, detail, and paint the landing gear struts identically to those on the P-40B Flying Tiger model (Chapter 8). Make a brake line from copper wire, bend it to shape, and glue it to the strut (fig. 9-13). Add more details to the main and tail wheel doors in the form of retraction struts using the reference photos as a guide (fig. 9-14). Make a rudder horn from stretched sprue, bend it around a paintbrush handle, cut it to fit, and cement it in place.

Replace the kit wheels and tires with True Details resin wheels for the early P-40s. Remove the tires from their mold plug with a razor saw. Drill new mounting holes into the inner hub to fit the kit axle. Paint and drybrush the wheels, but don't add them to the model until final assembly.

Don't use the kit windscreen and canopy. Use a Squadron canopy for the P-40B/C. Carefully cut out the parts. The canopies are very thin and fragile when cut out so some use care when handling them. Mask the canopy with 3M frosted transparent tape, then gently cut the tape away from the frames. Attach the windscreen to the fuselage using liquid cement. Use thinned Kristal Kleer to fill in any gaps. Mask off the inside of the windscreen, canopy, and cockpit interior and paint the clear parts Interior Green. You can

Next, make new tank sway braces and study photos to determine their proper location before attaching them. Drill four locating holes in the fuselage bottom for the braces. Make four braces from stretched sprue, flatten them with a pair of smooth, flat-jawed pliers. Leave the ends round. Insert the round end into the locating holes and cement them in place (fig. 9-11). Next, drill two holes in the top centerline of the belly tank about ⅛" apart using a no. 76 drill bit. Super glue two short

lengths of brass rod into the holes. Make sure they're straight. Match the tank up to the pylon and, where the two rods touch the pylon, mark and drill two additional holes.

Place the tank on the centerline bracket and mark and trim the sway braces where they touch the tank. Remove the tank from the pylon and drill four small holes for the sway braces' cross supports. Use small lengths of fine guitar string here, but almost any smaller-diameter sprue or

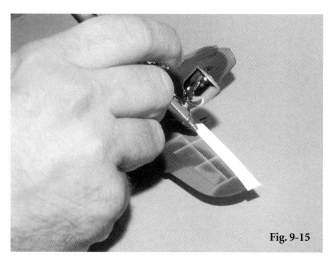

Fig. 9-15

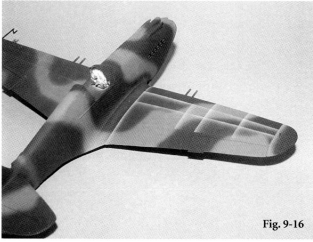

Fig. 9-16

use the kit rear quarter lights but don't add them until after you paint and decal the airframe.

Painting. We chose the paint scheme and markings for this project from AeroMaster Decal Sheet 48-056, Foreign Tomahawk Collection. The decal sheet provides the Sky fuselage band for the rear, but it doesn't match the Floquil British Sky Type S used to paint the spinner. Paint the spinner and rear fuselage band and let them dry for a couple of days. Mask off the rear band with 1/8" Fineline tape and drafting tape. Mask off the wheel and flap wells and paint the underside Floquil Medium Sea Grey. After the paint dries, mask off the undersides of the horizontal stabilizers so you can spray the topside camouflage.

Spray Floquil British Dark Green and Ocean Grey, lightened slightly with a drop of white, onto the top side

of the model using the pattern provided on the decal instruction sheet. Lightly respray the dark green of the camouflage pattern separation line with unlightened paint. Repeat this with the Ocean Grey.

Create a thin wash, about 1 part paint to 5 parts thinner, of Model Master Camouflage Gray to highlight the panel lines using a forced panel line technique. Lay a Post-it note or Fineline drafting tape along a panel line and spray very lightly along the edge of the mask, putting half the paint on the mask and half on the model (fig. 9-15). Mask along the front, top, or inside of a panel line. Also remember to keep the panel line pattern identical from one side of the model to the other. This can be overdone easily, so go slowly and lightly. The gray paint should be transparent enough to let the base color show through. If necessary, re-

spray the panel lines with the base color to tone then down (fig. 9-16).

Next, add a few drops of white to the base colors and spray a light, transparent mist onto the centers of various panels to fade the base color. Fade the upper surfaces of the wings, horizontal stabilizers, and the fuselage spine a bit more than you would the vertical surfaces of the tail and fuselage (fig. 9-17).

Mask off and respray the lower half of the fuselage to give a hard edge to the upper and lower camouflage colors. Do any needed touching up at this time. Use Ocean Grey to force the panel lines on the undersides. These, however, don't get toned down with the base color. Lightly mist other minor panels and areas with the Ocean Grey to give them a slightly worn, dirty appearance (fig. 9-18).

Finally, paint the wing and cowl guns with Testor's Gunmetal. Mask off

Fig. 9-17

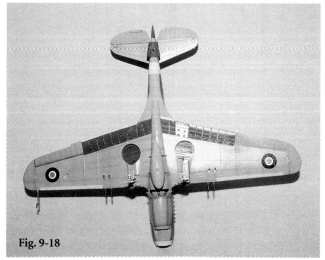

Fig. 9-18

Fig. 9-19

Gunpowder residue

Exhaust

Fig. 9-20

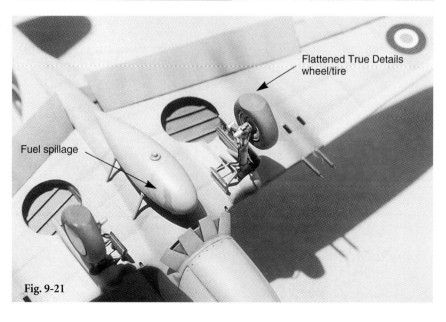

Flattened True Details
wheel/tire

Fuel spillage

Fig. 9-21

the leading edges of the wings and spray them Floquil USAAC Orange-Yellow. And mask off and paint the area around the exhausts AeroMaster Japanese Red-Brown. When the paint is dry, give the model several light coats of Testor's Glosscote. Let the clear coat dry for 48 hours before proceeding. Apply the decals using AeroMaster instructions and setting and solvent solutions.

Weathering. When the decals are dry, mix Grumbacher white and black oil paint, thinned with Turpenoid and apply it to the rescribed panel lines, control surfaces flap and wheel wells, landing gear, and the gear doors in a generous wash. Let this dry for 30 minutes and then gently wipe the excess away. After 24 hours, give the model an overall coat of Testor's Dullcote (fig. 9-19).

Now you can add details such as exhaust streaks, gunpowder residue, or dirt on the tires (fig. 9-20). You can simulate oil leaks by adding a small drop of thinned black oil paint to various locations around the spinner and engine cowls and gently wiping it off from front to back. The idea is to leave a slight streak on the paint, but not so much that it looks like the engine is coming apart. Minor leaks are okay, but anything beyond that implies combat damage or a serious maintenance problem. In either case, both would have to be fixed and cleaned up before normal flight operations could begin again. Add fuel spills to the belly tank with thinned, translucent burnt sienna oil paint. Put it on the top of the tank and then blow it down and back along the tank (fig. 9-21).

Final assembly. Remove the masks from the windscreen and canopy and add the M.V. lens to the landing light. Add the flaps, wheels, and a Teknics no. TK7207 Ring-and-Bead gunsight. Add aerial wires using fine nylon sewing thread attached with super glue and accelerator and paint them black.

10

WARHAWKS DOWN UNDER

The Monogram Pro-Modeler P-40E.
Model by Kevin Hjermstad

This kit is a reissue of an older Revell product from the 1970s. Monogram added some extra cockpit details, flattened tires, two different exhaust stacks, and crew figures. The lower wing assembly was warped on our kit. Quite noticeable is the general thickness of the kit parts, as are its raised panel lines. The kit rudder is also a bit oversized. Overall, the fit is not the best, so the kit is only of fair quality.

Assembly. You will have to add details to the cockpit and wheel wells and correct the rudder. You will also need to fade the paint and force the panel lines to achieve the look of a war-weary veteran of the South Pacific.

Cockpit. Out of the box, the cockpit is actually quite detailed, but it lacks depth, so spring it to life by adding some sheet styrene and sprue. By adding sheet plastic over the various kit panels, you can build up more relief to add wash to and drybrush. Cut some .010" sheet into the same shapes as some of the radio boxes and fuse panels and glue these on top of the kit parts. Drill no. 70 holes to simulate rivets in the panels (fig. 10-1).

Use the instrument panel straight out of the box. Paint it flat black and drybrush it with artist's black and white oil paint mixed to a medium gray. Use the artist's oils because they are more workable and mix with enamels. However, they take longer to dry. Pick out the instruments with white oil paint and a no. 000 brush. Add a drop of Kristal Kleer to each dial face to simulate the instrument glass.

The kit seat came with seat belts cast into the surface of the seat. Grind these off with a motorized tool fitted with a medium round bit. Detail the seat with strips of .010" plastic to simulate the stamped aluminum seat, using the photos provided in the kit instructions. Add True Details photoetched seat belts and paint them a combination of white and khaki with aluminum buckles. Detail the floor with stretched sprue and brass wire to simulate control cables going across the cockpit floor and the plumbing to the hydraulic pump.

Remove the throttle quadrant levers and cut shallow slots with a razor saw just deep enough to hold the new throttle levers. Make the throttle

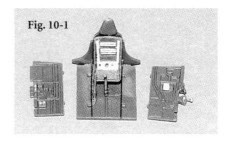

Fig. 10-1

levers from brass strip cut from an old photoetched fret. Then cut small strips to length and dab them with super glue to simulate the ends of the control knobs. Leave these off until final assembly because they are very delicate and could be broken off easily. Add brass wire to the base of the throttle quadrant to simulate the throttle and mixture control rods. Paint the entire assembly flat black and the control handles silver and brown.

Paint the cockpit Interior Green and the radio and fuse boxes flat black. Carefully apply a wash of burnt sienna oil paint and Turpinoid to the base of airframe ribbing, map cases, fuse panels, and any other recessed area. Next, make a drybrush mixture of white oil paint and Interior Green. Drybrush

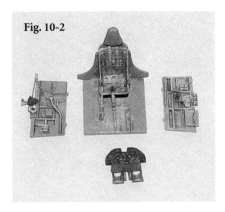

Fig. 10-2

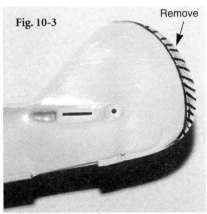

Fig. 10-3

Remove

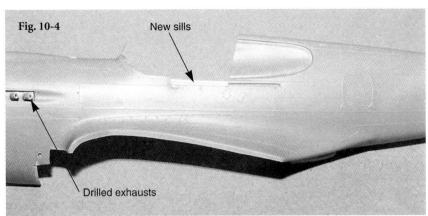

Fig. 10-4

New sills

Drilled exhausts

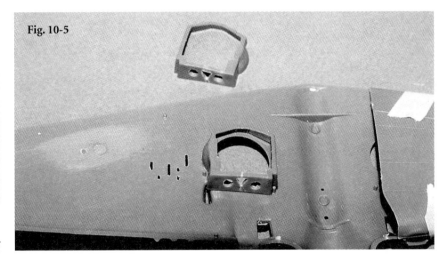

Fig. 10-5

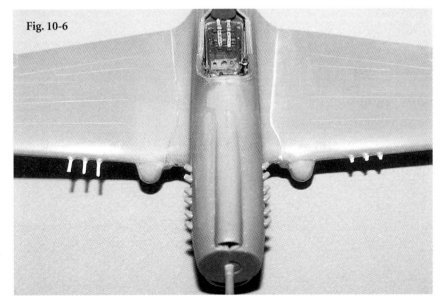

Fig. 10-6

this over the Interior Green portions of the cockpit and let it dry. Coat the entire cockpit, except the instrument panel, with Dullcote. After this dries, wipe a mix of brown and black pastels into the corners and around the cockpit to simulate dust and dirt (fig. 10-2).

Fuselage. The biggest error of the Monogram kit is its oversized rudder. Make a template out of paper and lay it on the inside of the kit rudder. Remove it by scribing the outline gently, cutting deeper with continuing passes until it was scribed through. Then laying the other half of the fuselage on the cut piece, use the corrected half as a template. Again, rescore the cut line until the piece is cut off. Sand the inside of the rudder to a taper so the halves are not too thick when they were assembled (fig. 10-3).

Drill out the exhausts with a no. 61 drill and cement them into the fuselage. Paint them a combination of flat black and rust.

Lastly, cut out the kit cockpit side walls and add a representation of the cockpit sills with .010 strip. Stack them

offset to replicate the sills of the airframe (fig. 10-4).

Cut out the overly thick cowl flaps and replace it with a piece of .020" styrene curved to match the fuselage. Scribe the cowl flaps individ-

ually on the plastic to simulate the individual flaps.

Mount the intake assembly into a fuselage half. Paint the intake divider and radiator steel and wash them with raw umber oil paint.

The fuselage assembly is pretty straightforward. Cut off the locating pins from both halves and sand them square on a piece of 400-grit sandpaper mounted on thick glass. This helps true the edges of the fuselage for a better fit. When the halves are ready to go together, secure them with masking tape. Keep a watchful eye on the intake assembly to make sure it doesn't twist as the cement dries.

Wings. The lower wing on our kit was severely warped. We reformed it while running it under warm water.

Begin by cutting three lightening holes in the forward portion of the wheel well box. Note the middle hole is triangular in shape. Use craft wire to simulate the hydraulic hoses in the wheel wells. Craft wire is a small-diameter, malleable wire found in craft stores (fig. 10-5).

Assemble the wings with the modified wheel wells. The fit on our kit was average on the wing edges. Sand the front edge with a Flex-i-File to keep a rounded shape. Sand the trailing edge with sanding sticks to cut down on its thickness and leave a cleaner edge.

Cut off the wing machine guns, leaving the protruding "bumps" on the wings. Sand these smooth and drill them with a no. 65 drill. Insert pieces of .035" styrene tubing into the holes and carefully drill them out with a no. 79 drill (fig. 10-6).

If your kit has large noticeable steps in the wing root as ours did, you will need to do a lot of sanding and filling with super glue. Trial fitting is the best way to reduce the amount of gaps needing filler. With most of the gaps eliminated, cement the aircraft wing and hold the dihedral in place with masking tape. Attach the rudder and elevator at this time and secure them with masking tape.

After these dry, add the fairing covers. You may need to do a lot of trial fitting to ensure a good fit. Cement them in place and let them dry. Fill them with super glue and blend them into the wing leading edge.

Finally, drill two cockpit vent holes in the wing root with a no. 70 drill bit.

Fig. 10-7

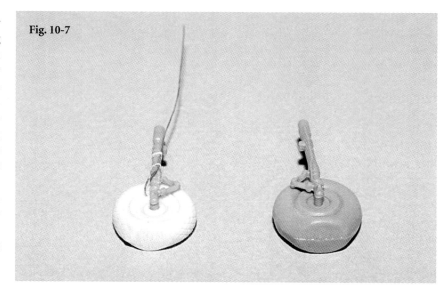

Fig. 10-8

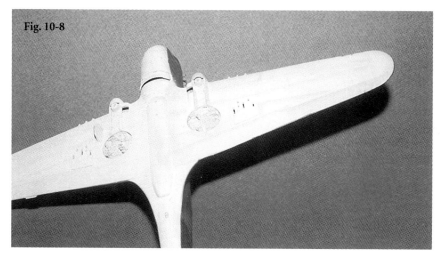

Detail parts. The kit struts come with molded brake hoses which you should remove with a sharp knife and file into a round shape with a sharp X-acto knife and needle files. Add a set of model railroad eyelets to the back of the struts for the brake hoses, then simulate hydraulic tubing with craft wire again. Use flat black paint to represent the rubber portion of the brake hose assembly.

Replace the kit wheels with the True Details resin wheels. The wheels do not fit on the kit strut spindle, so remove it and fashion a new one from brass tubing. Drill a small hole in the upper portion of the wheel hub of the resin tires to install the brake hose (fig. 10-7).

Paint these items but leave them off as sub-assemblies. Attach them after you paint, decal, and flat coat the major components.

Painting. After checking the model for any remaining seams or defects, begin painting. We used AeroMaster Warbird Colors Sky, Dark Earth, Dark Green, and Azure Blue for the camouflage and trim colors.

First paint the underside of the airframe Sky. When dry, mask off the demarcation line with 3M Fineline tape for the initial line and then 1" drafting tape to prevent overspray. After masking, respray the Sky along the tape edge to seal it. Doing so gives you a clean line when you spray the upper colors (fig. 10-8).

Then add the Dark Earth to the upper surfaces of the aircraft. Spray the Dark Green camouflage freehand onto the model following the painting

Fig. 10-9

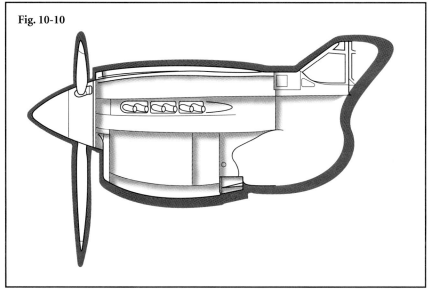

Fig. 10-10

or acrylic, are also usable.) Accent the underside of the aircraft with a light gray and the topside with medium gray. (Dark Gray was not used but would be used on all black or gray aircraft.) Spray a fine mist of medium gray along all the panel lines (fig. 10-10). Use Post-it correction tape for general masking and 3M Fineline tape for getting around compound curves. Lay the tape on the panel line. If it is a horizontal surface, such as a wing, you want the line of gray color to be sprayed towards the back and out away from the cockpit. On the fuselage the forced panel lines have to be aimed down and towards the back of the airframe. Be sure to duplicate everything from one side of the aircraft to the other, otherwise you end up with a patchwork of panels. The gray paint must be sprayed on very lightly, as it's easy to overdue the effect. You want to tint the underlying colors, not make a gray line. If the effect is too stark, you can respray the base color over the gray to tone it down. Also remember, the final flat coats tend to blend and slightly mute the effect, which is to your advantage.

After the paint thoroughly dries, apply a couple of coats of Testor's Glosscote to prepare for decaling.

Decals. The markings on our model came from Superscale decal sheet no. 48-550, P-40E Warhawk. Cut out the decals with an X-acto knife and small scissors. Most should go on with little trouble. If you have problems as we did with the flag nose art—a piece floated away as it was settling—maneuver it back into place and give everything three coats of Micro-Sol and Micro-Set. As each coat of decal setting solution dries, inspect the aircraft for air bubbles. Pierce them with a sharp knife tip and coat it again with Micro-Sol.

After all the decals are set and dry, tone down the markings to match the camouflage paint. After all, the paint is faded, so why not the decals? Begin by making a light gray mix of tinted thinner, not a mixture of paint to actually cover anything. Now very gently spray the tint onto the decal. Really back off on the paint mixture

references on the Superscale decal sheet and the Monogram kit instructions.

After the paint dries, start the weathering process by fading the paint. This will give the P-40 the worn, weather-beaten appearance of operational aircraft serving in the Southwest Pacific Theater. Start by adding a little white to the base color. The lightened color should not have too much contrast. A gradual transition is desired. Spray the lightened mixture into the center of the panel. It should cover the center part of a panel but not the edges. They should remain the standard color. Each color has to be done and it helps if the small access panels

such as oil tank covers, gun bay covers, and handholds are faded individually too. These can be masked off with drafting tape, Post-it Notes, or Post-it correction tape (fig. 10-9).

Now, because the Monogram kit has raised panel lines and many were lost filling seams, paint will help replicate them so they appear as though they are there. A favorite method among modelers is called forcing panel lines. you will use two or three types of gray paint to do this type of panel accenting on this model. We used Gunze Sangyo no. 61 IJN Light Gray, no. 53 Neutral Gray, and no. 333 Extra Dark Sea Gray (other brands, enamel

on your airbrush; you don't want gray colored decals. When you see a slight reduction in your decals luminosity—stop. Now your decals don't look brand new while the rest of the airframe looks faded. After you have completed this last step, coat the model with three or four coats of Dullcote to seal and homogenize the surface (fig. 10-11).

Weathering. Ah, weathering. This is many modelers' favorite part of model building. Nothing makes some of us happier then to take a pretty little airplane and make it look like it just parked on the grass after a hard sortie.

Aircraft weathering generally takes four different steps: fading the paint, creating oil and hydraulic leaks, scuffing and chipping paint, and making gun and exhaust stains. You've already faded the paint and decals earlier, so now you can concentrate on the other areas.

Create oil and hydraulic leaks with a wash. Oil paints flow nicely and are easy to work with to create this effect. Mix raw umber and wash the landing gear struts and wheel hubs. Streak the oils downward but don't cover the oleo strut, as this should remain clean and shiny.

Fluids leak out of access panels, refueling caps, and wheel wells. A couple of streaks behind an access panel add interest to the model. Take a small brush and put a small dab of oil behind the access cover, then use your finger to wipe back towards the tail. You should see a little streak moving down the airframe. Add the streaks to various areas of the airframe, using operational photos to determine the areas where these occurred most. As with most weathering, don't overdue it. Remember your aircraft has to remain airworthy (fig. 10-12).

Create the look of scuffed and chipped paint by mixing silver enamel with raw umber oil paint. Silver paint is too bright and stark by itself, but the deep brown color of the oils mute this. It also makes the silver paint easier to blend. Combine the paints in about a 1:1 ration with just a little more silver than raw umber.

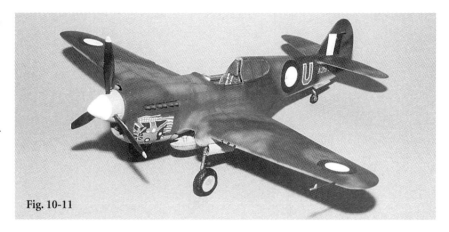

Fig. 10-11

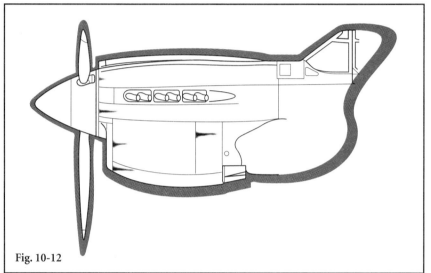

Fig. 10-12

Fig. 10-13

Paint chips are mainly to the areas of prop wash: cowling, wing leading edges, and tailplane leading edges. All are places where dirt and other debris are kicked up by the prop blade. Mask the panel lines with a Post-it note or

Fig. 10-14

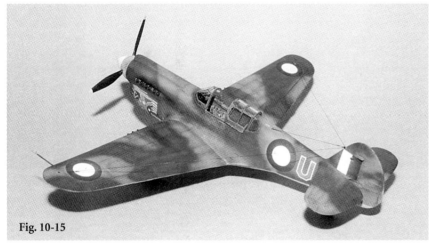

Fig. 10-15

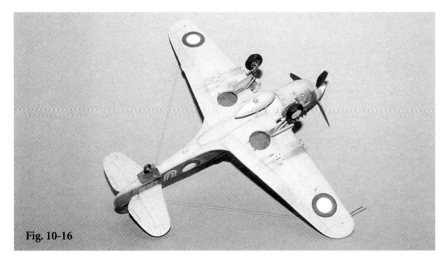

Fig. 10-16

panel and as if the paint is placed on top of the model. If you separate the paint applications, the chipping looks uneven and more realistic (fig. 10-13).

Scuffed paint is usually caused by the ground crew and pilot walking on the aircraft, either doing maintenance or getting in the cockpit. The paint is often scuffed on wing walks, cockpits, and gunbay access doors. To scuff the paint, apply the paint combination along a panel line. Using a Q-tip, gently stroke across the paint. The oil in the paint will blend and feather out into the upper surface, leaving a worn mark. Push the paint into adjoining panels but don't go too far away from the main traffic areas. Using this medium, you can even make the transition from scuffed to chipped paint (fig. 10-14).

Use pastels to create streaks from gunfire and exhaust smoke. Shave off black and brown chalk with an X-acto knife into a couple of piles. Add a small amount of brown to the black for the exhausts. Apply this with a no. 1 brush by rubbing them into the exhausts and then streaking them down the fuselage. Use the black pastel again, but with even less brown for the gun streaking. Also apply it to the shell ejection chutes and streak it back towards the tail section (figs. 10-15 and 10-16).

Final assembly. Polish the kit canopy with Blue Magic compound. Apply this with pieces of T-shirt and buff it out. Then dip the entire canopy in Future Floor Wax. Then place the parts on a napkin and cover them with a bowl to protect the pieces from dust while they dry for at least 24 hours.

Then mask the dry canopy pieces with Blenderm, a hospital first aid tape. Spray the Interior Green color on first. After this dries, spray dark green over the canopy. Lastly, give all the canopy components a flat coat. Then attach them with Testor's canopy cement.

Fabricate a new gunsight out of scrap plastic pieces to replace the piece of clear sheet styrene attached as the gunsight glass.

On the underside of the aircraft is a large landing light. Drill this out with

tape. Then, using a brush, dab the paint mixture along the tape line. Reverse the tape and repeat the process. Why not just dabble the brush along the panel line? This tends to look too even on both sides of the

a motorized tool using a cone-shaped bit. Insert an M.V. lens no. 116 into the cavity and attach it with super glue (fig. 10-17).

Detail the kit drop tank with wire and mount it onto the underside. Super glue the kit braces in place. After these dry, add pieces of stretched sprue to the braces to simulate the turnbuckles that mount between the brace and fuel tank.

Make the antenna wire from Invisible Thread, sometimes called Tailor's Thread. Drill no. 76 holes where the wires will be placed. Put a drop of super glue on the end of the thread and insert it into the hole. Now touch the hole with a drop of accelerator to instantly freeze the join. Then string the wire to the other hole, keep it taut, and attach it with the same method. Paint the wires flat black after they are mounted. Add drops of Kristal Kleer on wire ends for the insulators.

Fig. 10-17

11
OPERATION TORCH

P-40F conversion. Model by Glen Phillips

In the early 1990s, WW II aircraft modelers were blessed with a brand new P-40N kit from the Mauve company of Japan. This was the first fully original injection-molded kit released by this company in the United States. Their previous releases had been mixed-media conversions of other kits. They were not without their problems and they were very expensive. The P-40N came as a pleasant surprise to most and was quickly followed by a Royal Air Force Kittyhawk III (P-40M) in an RAF desert scheme. The only real change from the N model were new parts for the fuselage decking behind the cockpit and the decals. Then Mauve changed the color of the plastic and added new decals to create the P-40M. This kit forms the basis for this conversion.

The kit is molded in a dark olive plastic and has about 75 parts. It has many finely recessed panel lines, but there are no rivets to be seen. Mauve also molded the correct offset to the vertical fin. For the most part, the primary parts fit like a glove, although some of the smaller parts have glitches.

The second part of this conversion is a P-40F/L conversion kit by AeroMaster. The conversion parts consist of a new nose, vertical fin, rudder, and flaps. The vertical fin and rudder are provided for modelers wishing to make a short-tailed P-40F. Since this project is a long-tailed version, these parts will not be used. Also, set the flaps aside for another project. Aero-Master's instructions are fairly simple and state that a careful job of removing the nose from the Mauve kit will result

in little, if any, need for filler. Were they right? Read on.

We built this model, like all projects, in a series of what we hope are logical phases, all designed to ease or speed assembly. While we used the instruction sheet as a general reference, project requirements often dictated a diversion from Mauve's assembly steps. **Preparing the conversion parts.** Begin the conversion by carefully removing the nose from the fuselage. Do this with a series of fine cuts with a new no. 11 knife blade and a razor saw. After several passes with the knife and saw, snap the nose away from the fuselage. Remove any burrs with a sanding stick. The key is to work slowly and carefully. If it takes a few extra minutes, so be it. The alternative is spending a lot more time later aligning, filling, and sanding

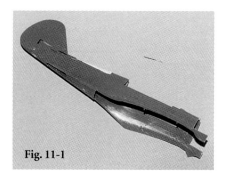
Fig. 11-1

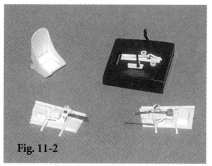
Fig. 11-2

repairs. Remember, you're not required to build a model from start to finish in a weekend.

Next, temporarily tack the fuselage shells together with tape and check the fit of the nose. The only thing interfering with the fit on our kit were bits of excess resin in some of the corners and along the edge of one side. Once these were cleaned out, the fit was very good. AeroMaster is right. Set these parts aside for later (fig. 11-1).

Cockpit. If the Mauve kit has one failing, it's the cockpit interior. Not that Mauve didn't try. The kit features a separate floor, stick, hydraulic pump handle, instrument panel, cockpit side panels, rudder pedals, and seat. Discard the kit seat and cockpit side panels, since the seat looks more like boiler plate than sheet metal, and the side walls, while a nice thought, lack relief and only vaguely resemble those of the P-40N they were originally designed for.

So, this project has evolved into an exercise in cockpit detailing using only plastic sheet, rod, strip, and sprue. Start by cutting out a new set of side walls from .010" sheet plastic using the kit parts as a pattern. Next, and using reference photos as a guide, sketch the cockpit structure and interior components on the plastic using a soft pencil. This gives you an idea of not only where things go but approximately what size they will be. Use Evergreen Strip Styrene to make the ribs and stringers in the cockpit and make other parts from various sizes of plastic cut to shape. Use plastic rod in assorted diameters to make the oxygen regulator, trim knobs, cowl flap control, and the flap and landing gear control handles. Use thicker pieces of plastic to

make radios, the map case, electrical boxes, throttle quadrant, etc. Make an oxygen hose from flexible, insulated electrical wire. A thin wafer of rod and a piece of sprue replicate the canopy crank (fig. 11-2). When completed, cement the new side walls in place in the fuselage. Spray them Testor's Model Master Interior Green, give them a black wash, and drybrush them with Testor's Zinc Chromate. Paint the individual components on the side walls flat black and drybrush them with dark gray. Paint the landing gear and flap handles flat red and flat yellow respectively (fig. 11-3).

Tackle the seat and rear bulkhead next. Discard the kit seat and build a new one from .010" sheet plastic using reference photos as a guide. The seat should represent the round-back styles seen in the earlier Warhawks. Paint the seat Humbrol Flat Aluminum. Make the seat belts from masking tape and thin wafers of plastic and paint them an off-white color with a hint of tan. Paint the buckles Flat Aluminum. Make new vertical seat supports for the rear bulkhead with styrene rod. Use a second, smaller piece for the transverse

bar near the top of the seat supports. Paint the bulkhead and supports Interior Green, give them a black wash and light drybrush them with Zinc Chromate Green and Flat Aluminum. Set these components aside.

The cockpit floor is the upper surface of the wing and Mauve correctly molded it with a gentle curve. It lacks a lot of the other details however. Add a center flange down the middle of the floor to represent the area where the wings are joined together. Add thin sections of styrene tubing to the floor to represent the main and auxiliary wing tank fuel gauges. Use the kit control stick and use various sections of plastic rod for the aileron and elevator control rods and the stick limiter. Make another piece of rod into the hydraulic pump on the floor. Cement the kit pump handle to the top of it. Use the kit rudder pedals as they are. Paint most of this Interior Green and give it the wash and drybrush treatment to pop out the details. Paint the fuel gauges flat black with a drop of clear gloss in the centers. Set this assembly aside.

Although Mauve provided a really well-done instrument panel, the upper shape of the panel bears no relation to the inner curvature of the fuselage. Plan on some trimming and shimming to get it to fit. Modify the lower sub panel a bit, using the reference photos to bring it more in line with the earlier P 40 E/F panels. Paint the panel flat black and then drybrush it with a dark gray. Use a white Eagle Prismacolor pencil with a sharp point to pick out

Fig. 11-3

the details in the dials. Use a silver-colored pencil to pick out the various switches and small knobs on the panel. Place a small drop of Microscale Micro Gloss onto the instrument faces to represent glass. Set the instrument panel aside.

Fuselage. Once the cockpit components are completed, it's time to start on the fuselage and the meat of this conversion. First, carve out the flashed-over square hole at the base of the rudder. Next, test the fit of the fuselage at the notch for the offset vertical stabilizer. It may need a little trimming to get it to fit right. When everything has come together, cement the fuselage shells together.

When the two fuselage halves have set, you can test-fit the new resin nose. Use the resin nose to set the width of the fuselage shells. When the fit is satisfactory, super glue the nose in place. Use the super glue sparingly at first, and where possible, try to add the glue to the inside coming up from the wing bay. Neatness counts, as it usually saves a lot of time later. Note that the fuselage with the resin nose in place is now very unbalanced. Keep a relatively firm hand on it at all times. Otherwise you run the risk of it flipping out of your hand, and it is likely to land nose down. If it hits something hard the lip of the intake will chip (fig. 11-4).

Next, add the rear cockpit shroud from the top. It rests on a pair of rails molded to the inside of the fuselage. While the cement is setting, test-fit the clear canopy quarterlight section (part D3). Make any adjustments to the width of the fuselage that are necessary while the interior shroud is setting. Once it has set, you won't be able to pinch or widen the fuselage to match the clear part. Lightly clamp everything in position until the glue has set. When it's dry, remove the glass part and set it aside.

Next, add the instrument panel from the underside. As previously mentioned, the fit is less than perfect. You can use Micro Kristal Kleer or a thick, fast-setting white glue to tack the panel in place. The working time of this glue will let you make any

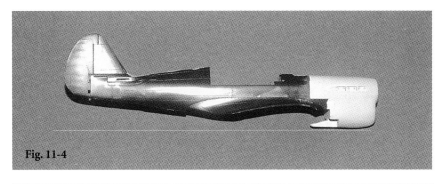

Fig. 11-4

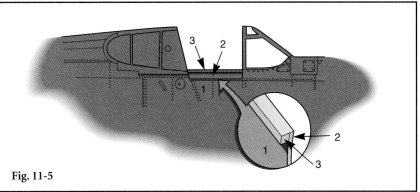

Fig. 11-5

necessary adjustments. When everything is squared, a couple of drops of super glue on the back of the joint will secure the panel .

Now add the floor assembly. Tack the rear bulkhead in place and set the floor into position from the wing bay. Four locating nubs are provided to ensure proper alignment. Make any adjustments in the fore-and-aft rake of the rear bulkhead. Cement the floor in place and hold it in position for a few minutes.

Once the floor is in place, add new cockpit sills. Although many kits have been issued with separated canopies, many kit manufacturers still intend for the canopies to be closed. They tend to ignore the sill area. Mauve was no exception with this kit. Pop the clear part D3 back in place and measure the distance to the front of the cockpit sill (about 15 mm long and 1.5 mm deep). Cut two strips of .020" sheet plastic to the proper dimensions and cement in place. Add a small piece of strip to the top of the sill. Use the reference photos as a guide (fig. 11-5).

Wings. Before cementing the wing halves together, you must first add the ribs and spars that form the wheel well. Note the outer portion of the cockpit

floor serves as the inner rib although it lacks any detail. Cement these parts in place. Paint these parts either Interior Green or Zinc Chromate Green, wash them, and when dry, drybrush them. Don't forget to paint the outer panels of the cockpit floor.

Next, test-fit the upper wing parts to the lower wing. Make sure the trailing edges of the wings behind the wheel wells come together without any undue pressure. You might need to lightly sand the tops of the ribs and spars (especially parts A7 and A8) around the wheel wells in order for the wings to fit together. Cement the wings together and lightly clamp them in place for a few minutes. Don't use too much pressure on the trailing edges or you may distort them. When dry, remove the seam with a light sanding. Pay particular attention to the front of the landing gear pod. You may need a small spot of filler. Finally, drill out the machine gun barrels.

When the wings are dry, test-fit them to the fuselage. You might need to wiggle the wings into place under the resin nose carburetor fairing. If there is a small gap between the carb fairing and underside of the wings, fill it. Overall, the fit of the parts on our model was pretty good, so there were no major problems. Align the wings from the front, back, and top and hold them in position with tape or rubber bands. Use a fine brush or ruling pen to flow liquid cement into the joints, letting capillary action take the cement along the seam. Take care of any seams when the glue is dry (figs. 11-6 and 11-7).

Detail parts. Now add the rear canopy quarterlights to the fuselage. The fit should be almost perfect with little seam work required. Add the horizontal stabilizers to the fuselage, the rudder horn to the left side of the vertical fin, and the pitot tube to the left wing.

The wheels and tires in the kit are something of a let-down. The tires have a diamond tread but have flat sides and an under-sized wheel cover that stands out from the surface. Use True Details resin wheels for the P-40E-M instead. These wheels have the correct diameter wheel cover and sharply molded diamond tread. If anything, the side walls are a little too bulged (they look like they're low on air), but this is easily fixed with a sanding stick. Drill holes for the brake lines inside the landing gear pod and the inner face of wheel hub.

AeroMaster's conversion instructions say to use the kit cowl flaps. Well, that's true to a point, but there's more to it. Allison-powered P-40s had a ring of four cowl flaps arranged around the aft bottom portion of the lower cowl. All four cowl flaps were positioned alongside each other (see the reference photos). Merlin-powered P-40s had the cowl flaps arranged in two groups

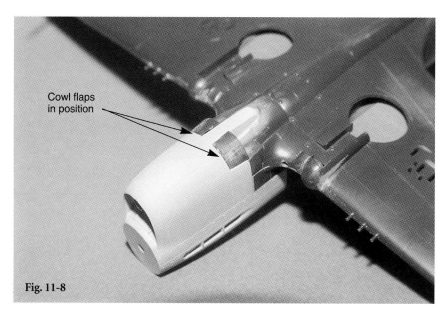

Cowl flaps in position

Fig. 11-8

of two, split by the carburetor intake ducting. Split the kit cowl flaps (part C22) in to two parts and fill in the old panel lines and sand them smooth. Then reverse the flaps and scribe new lines. Super glue these parts to the back of the resin nose (fig. 11-8).

Super glue the kit exhaust stacks to the resin nose. It will help if you sand down the mounting pegs on the exhausts a bit, otherwise the base of the stack will stand away from the cowl leaving a weak joint. Alternatively, drill deeper mounting holes in the resin nose. It's your call. Start from the back and work your way forward. Use a slower-setting super glue so you have time to align the stacks.

Assemble the spinner but don't add the propeller blades. Go easy with the cement. Also add the antenna mast to the fuselage spine.

Painting. Prior to painting, give the model a quick examination and take care of any visible seams, sanding marks, etc. Mask off the rear canopy quarterlights leaving the vertical frame members bare. Also mask off the other canopy parts. Stuff some facial tissue into the cockpit and main- and tail-wheel wells.

Paint the model with AeroMaster's enamel-based Warbirds Colors—specifically, RAF Dark Earth, Mid-Stone, and Azure Blue. Use the Mid-Stone first and let it dry for about an hour. Lightly draw the upper surface camouflage pattern on the surface with a pencil. Then spray the Dark Earth free-hand using the pencil lines as a guide. Next spray the Azure Blue. Add a few drops of AeroMaster White to a fresh batch of Mid-Stone and then spray it into the middle of all the major

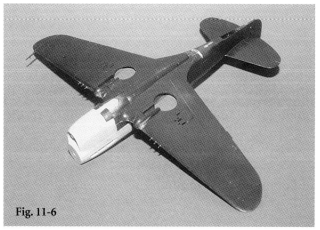

Fig. 11-6

Fig. 11-7

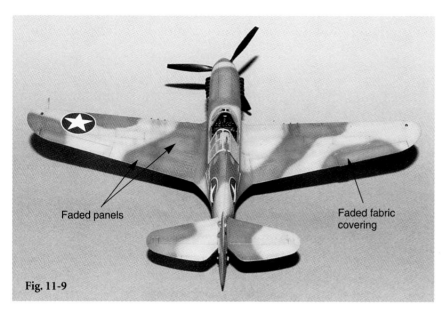

Faded panels

Faded fabric covering

Fig. 11-9

panels and control surfaces using the panel lines (not the rivets) as a guide. Repeat this process for the Dark Earth and Azure Blue. Add a couple more drops of white to each color and spray each onto the fabric control surfaces to simulate the increased fade rate of fabric over metal. Don't forget to paint the spinner, canopies, and landing gear doors their appropriate colors. Paint the exhausts Floquil Bronze. As a side note, the photo on which this model was based appeared in two publications. Only one commented on the color of the spinner, noting that it was Dark Earth. It could, however be red, which was a common theater recognition color in use in North Africa and the Mediterranean. We painted our spinner Dark Earth. When the paint is dry, add a clear gloss coat (fig. 11-9).

Decals. The decals were a problem for us. The instructions in AeroMaster's conversion set list a series of decal sheets specifically for P-40F and L aircraft. Great. Unfortunately, they weren't released yet. We resorted to the spares box and a looked at a lot of photos as a reference. We needed a photo showing the camouflage pattern, the national insignia, serial number, and nose art. We also needed to know the colors to use. Fortunately, we found such a photo on page 68 of Bunrin-Do's *Famous Airplanes of the World #39, Curtiss P-40 Warhawk.* We chose the United States insignia and flag

from Accurate Miniature's P-51 kit and the yellow serial numbers from AeroMaster's 48-051, U.S. 45-Degree ID Numbers and Letters (Yellow). The name "DAMMIT" came from Super Scale 13-11, U.S. Armor Insignia and Codes (White), 1/35 scale. We individually cut out and applied the numbers and letter in the serial and name. Make sure you have lots of time for this. Also take care to keep everything going in a straight line along the aircraft's datum line. When the decals dry, given them a light coat of Dullcote.

Weathering. You've already partially weathered it by fading the paint as you applied it. The marking needs to be

faded as well. National insignia, serial numbers, squadron codes, etc., can look very out of place if they're fresh and new-looking on an airplane that has been heavily weathered. With that in mind, add 3 to 4 drops of Testor's Model Master Light Gull Gray into the airbrush with a color cup about half full of thinner. Spray this mixture, essentially a sprayed wash, onto the decals to tone them down. Spray the most on the markings on the upper wings, a little less on the fuselage, and just enough to kill the newness on the undersides. Put a bit more of the wash on the fuselage markings on the upper third than on the lower sections.

Create the look of paint chips with Humbrol Flat Aluminum and a silver-colored pencil. Accentuate the control and panel lines by applying a mix of black and brown watercolor with a fine-tipped brush.

Next, apply the exhaust and gun soot. Use a very dark gray paint for this rather than black. Black is too dark and rather stark looking. Besides, sooty black exhausts stains are a sign of engine problems. Also add some stains to the underside of the belly. Airplanes leak all kinds of fluids and a combination of gravity and air flow blow most of them back along the belly of the aircraft (fig. 11-10).

Final assembly. Paint the landing gear struts and tires next. The axle shafts on

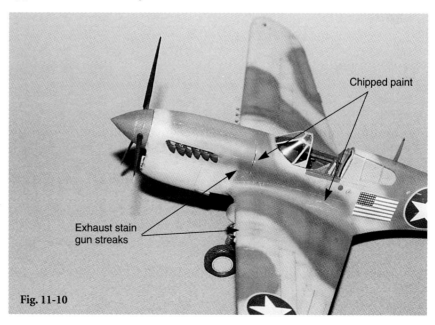

Chipped paint

Exhaust stain gun streaks

Fig. 11-10

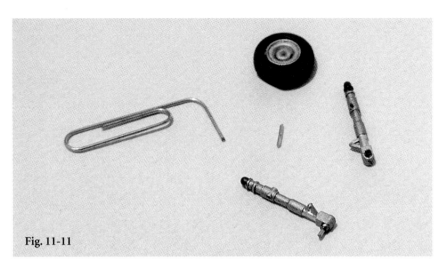

Fig. 11-11

Clean the mold line off the gunsight's reflector glass. Paint and add the gunsight into the cockpit. Note that the large square cutout in the instrument panel for the gunsight seems to have no relation to the small round peg on the sight itself. You can cement the gunsight to a larger piece of plastic and insert it into the hole. Then cement the windscreen in place with Kristal Kleer

If you add the drop tank, note that the sway braces don't exactly match up with the holes on the tank. The braces are too wide, so you may want to shorten the inner braces to close them up a bit. Mauve (and everyone else it seems) also forgot to add the drop tank's pylon, which is what the drop tank was actually fastened to. The sway braces just kept the tank from swaying. Replicate the pylon with a small piece of strip styrene, the ends rounded off and cemented in place. Paint it flat aluminum (fig. 11-12).

Paint the back side of the landing light bright silver. Then cement the clear parts representing the formation and navigation lights and the landing light in place with Kristal Kleer. When dry, paint the wing lights a gloss red (left) and gloss dark blue or dark green (right). Rig the antenna wire and the project is complete. You can almost feel the desert heat (fig. 11-13).

the struts of our model were too short for the True Details wheels. The tire side wall was contacting the strut before the shaft met the hub. To remedy this, we set a piece of paper clip wire into an appropriately sized hole and super glued it in place. We drilled the same size hole into the center of the wheel hub. Then we super glued the struts and tail wheel into the wings and fuselage respectively, and after they set, we tacked the wheels on with Kristal Kleer (fig. 11-11).

When the glue has hardened up a little, set the model on its wheels and rotate the tires until the contact patch is flat on the ground. Put super glue on the tip of a paper clip and apply it to the wheel hub to lock the wheels in

place. Use fine, dark-colored wire for the brake lines. Next, add the landing gear doors.

Paint the inside area of the radiator intake flat black and drybrush it with Humbrol no. 53 Gunmetal. Touch up the inner surfaces of the intake lips with the exterior camouflage colors, and when dry, give the entire inner radiator area a dark wash.

Paint the prop blades flat black and drybrush them well with a dark gray. Paint the tips flat yellow. When dry, cement the blades into the spinner. Sand down the locating pins if necessary to clear the holes. Note the flat pitch of the blades. If you want a coarser pitch, remove the locating pins completely and twist the blades accordingly.

Tank pylon

Fig. 11-12

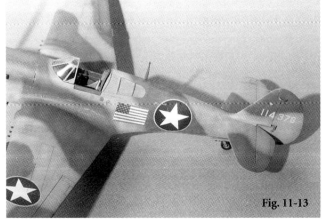

Fig. 11-13

12

SOUTH AFRICA IN NORTH AFRICA

Building a P-40K. Model by Glen Phillips

For this conversion, use the ancient and somewhat venerable 1/48 scale Otaki P-40E along with a Medallion Models P-40K resin conversion set. The Otaki kit has been around for 20 years or more and has also been reissued under the Arii and AMT labels. The kit features engraved panel lines and a bazillion countersunk rivets. When first issued, it was considered a great advance over the Monogram kits of the day.

Well, times have changed. The Otaki kit is now very long in the tooth. The engraved detail is too deep and prominent, the cockpit detail is inadequate, and the wings have too much sweep back on the leading edges. There's more, but none of it is insurmountable.

Medallion's P-40K conversion set has also been around for a while, though not nearly as long as the Otaki kit. The conversion is specifically made for the Otaki kit. It looks as though the master pattern was made by hacking off the tail of the Otaki kit and making the appropriate modifications. It may fit other 1/48 scale P-40 kits, but don't bet your airbrush on it. If there is anything wrong with the conversion, it's that it lacks the characteristic hump on the front of the vertical fin cap. That can be fixed easily.

Assembly. Begin the conversion by cutting the tail off both kit fuselage halves. Medallion provides specific instructions on where to cut (1⁵⁄₈" forward from the rudder post). Make sure the cuts are as straight and square

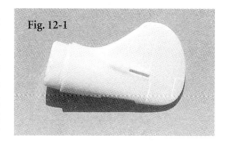

Fig. 12-1

as you can possibly make them. You will save yourself a lot of filling and sanding later.

Remove the excess resin plug from the conversion tail piece and discard it. Next, drill a small hole in the tail wheel well for the kit tail wheel strut. Medallion did not hollow out the tail wheel well, so if you want to add additional detailing inside it, you have your work cut out for you. Also, look into the horizontal stabilizer mounting slots. If you see bits of resin, clean them out and test-fit the stabilizers. Make any necessary trimming adjustments at this time but don't cement the stabilizers in place. Next, take a small piece of stretched sprue and super glue it to the upper front portion of the fin cap. Let it set for a minute or so, and then fair it in with your favorite filler. We used Tamiya Putty. When the filler is dry, carefully reshape the fin cap to restore the humped appearance that is characteristic of the early P-40K tails (fig. 12-2).

Cockpit. Most aircraft kits begin with the cockpit and this one is no exception. Make this model with a closed canopy so you can concentrate on the conversion and not worry about whether the tick marks on the instrument dials are in scale. However, there is a lot that is visible through the greenhouse canopy, and that cockpit sure could use some work. So, we suggest you use Shep Paine's time-honored "creative gizmology" (see Kalmbach Book's *Modeling Tanks and Military Vehicles* by Shepard Paine) and break the cockpit components down into basic shapes which can be easily replicated with plastic sheet, rod, and sprue. Use the kit cockpit floor, seat, and instrument panel. Remove all other detail, including what is on the cockpit side walls.

Add a few pieces of strip styrene to both cockpit side walls to represent the internal structure of the cockpit. Use additional bits of sheet, strip and rod to make the trim knobs, landing and flap control, the throttle quadrant, radios, cockpit lights, cowl flap control handle, canopy crank, map case, oxygen regulator, and the hydraulic pump lever. Again, break the parts down into their basic shapes. You don't need to reproduce every little angle, curve, nut, and bolt because the canopy is closed. Paint the walls and main structural elements were painted Testor's Model Master Interior Green, give them a black wash, and drybrush them with Testor's Model Master Zinc Chromate. Paint most of the add-on components flat black and drybrush them with a dark gray (fig. 12-2).

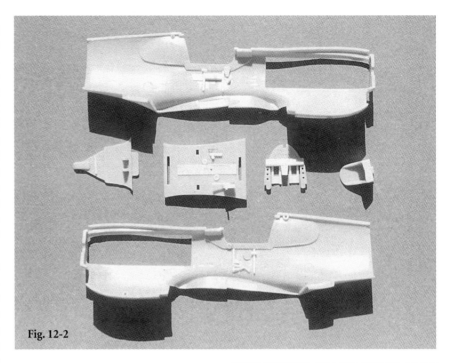

Fig. 12-2

Make new rudder pedals from strip plastic and cement them to a pair of rods hanging from the back of the instrument panel (fig. 12-3). Paint the pedals and rods Interior Green and drybrush them with a bit of Humbrol no. 56 Flat Aluminum (although any similar color would work just as well). Give the instrument panel a new lower sub-panel, paint it flat black, and then drybrush it with a dark gray. Put a drop of clear gloss on the faces of the instruments.

Use the kit control stick, but make the elevator and aileron control rods and the limiter bar from plastic rod. Add two thin wafers of sprue to the floor and paint them gloss black. These represent the fuel gauges. Reshape the seat and make masking tape seat belts with painted buckles.

Assemble the engine, engine mounts, and firewall, but don't paint them. Seal this assembly up inside the cowling but it still serves as the mount for the propeller. Set the cockpit floor and engine assembly aside for later.

Fuselage. Now the fun begins. Dry-fit the two fuselage halves together and check the fit of the new tail. If your saw cuts are good, there should be minimal gaps and the parts should be fairly well in line with each other. Make any necessary adjustments. If the fuselage is

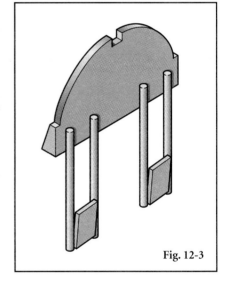

Fig. 12-3

too narrow, shim it with thin sheet stock. If it is too wide, gently sand the mating surfaces from the cockpit and wing cut out to the saw cuts. Test-fit often and resist the temptation to charge in with coarse files to make the job go faster.

When you are satisfied with the fit and alignment, cement the two fuselage halves together. Use care to ensure a proper alignment. When the parts are set, add the new resin tail with super glue. We used a little Micro Kristal Kleer to set it in place because it dries slowly and allows plenty of time for adjustments. Use a pair of rigid

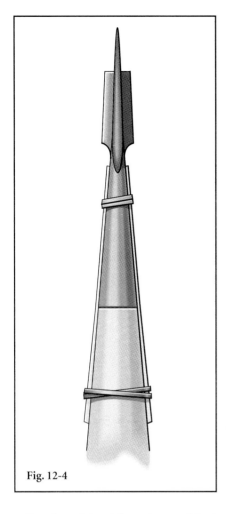

Fig. 12-4

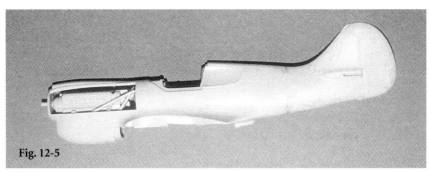

Fig. 12-5

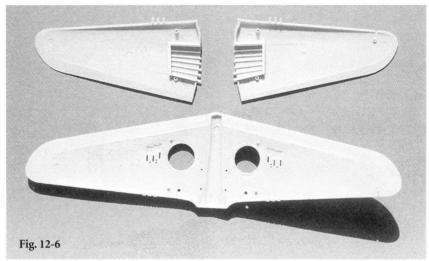

Fig. 12-6

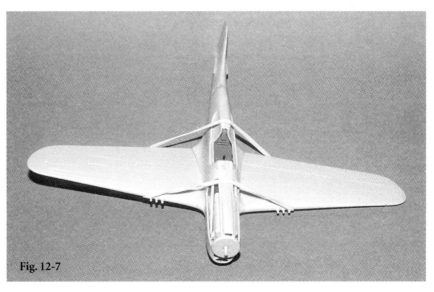

Fig. 12-7

splints (popsicle sticks or brass tubing) held in place with rubber bands to maintain the alignment while the Kristal Kleer dries (fig. 12-4). When it is dry, there is still enough "give" so you can make minor adjustments if necessary. When you are satisfied with the alignment, use super glue to finally anchor the resin part in position. Remove any excess super glue within a few hours. Use filler and sanding sticks to erase the seam. It may help to shoot some gray primer paint on the joint to help you identify small gaps or pits. Now you can add the cockpit floor and engine assembly (fig. 12-5).

Wings. Remove the round wheel wells molded to the bottom of the wing with a motorized tool and clean the area with files and sand paper. Next, box in the wheel wells with strip plastic to represent the wing ribs and front and rear spar. Cement these to the upper wing after first measuring and drawing in their proper position. Then cement smaller strips of plastic to the upper wing to represent the stringers under the upper wing skin (fig. 12-6). Paint the entire area Interior Green, give it a black wash, and drybrush it with Zinc Chromate Green. Then cement the upper and lower wing components together. When the parts are dry, rub down the leading and trailing edges and drill out the gun barrels. Then cement the wing to the fuselage and fill any gaps or seams (fig. 12-7).

Detail parts. Use the set of exhausts in Medallion's conversion kit because the ones in the kit are abysmal. Clean them up, paint the bases flat black and super glue them into position in the cowl panels. Cement the cowl panels in place. The fit on ours was pretty good. All of the seams fall on natural panel lines, so go easy with the cement. If it bubbles out of the seam, you'll have to remove it later and probably need to restore the panel lines as well (fig. 12-8).

Mount the cowl flaps in the closed position, but the raised lines will get removed so you'll need to rescribed new ones.

The wheel pods are not exactly accurate, but with some cleaning up and test-fitting they'll look fine. Square off the front door and cement the pods into place. Make sure the pods and the fuselage are all pointing in the same direction as viewed from the bottom (fig. 12-9).

One other thing you must change is the landing gear door. It's not even close. Cut off the kit door and make two new ones for each pod from Evergreen ½" styrene tubing. Cut a piece of tubing to the proper length (⅝") for the long door, and then cut lengthwise into smaller sections (³⁄₁₆") to make the door. Make the smaller inner doors the same way with the proper adjustment for length (¼"). Cement the doors firmly in place and paint them with the rest of the airframe (fig. 12-10).

Discard the kit wheels, as their hubs are the wrong size in diameter and depth. Add new wheels from the AMT/ERTL P-40N kit (which received a pair of aftermarket late N wheels). AMT/ERTL's wheels are also not quite correct because the hub covers are too prominent. Sand these down and drill in the four hub cover mounting bolts with a fine drill bit. Use a dark-colored wire to replicate brake lines. Add these to pre-drilled holes in the landing gear pod and the inner surface of the wheel hub. Now, add the horizontal stabilizers if you haven't already done so (fig. 12-11).

Painting. Give the model a final check to make sure you didn't miss anything.

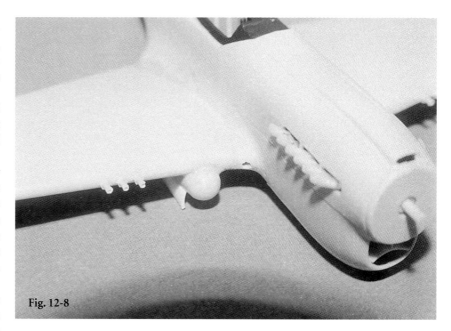
Fig. 12-8

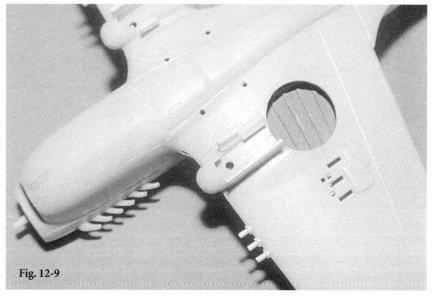
Fig. 12-9

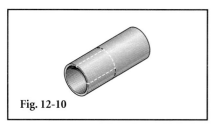
Fig. 12-10

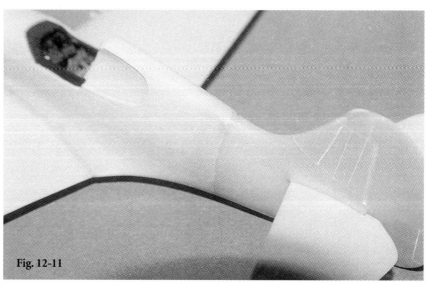
Fig. 12-11

Fig. 12-12

Sometimes it helps to do this a few days after you've completed it and you think you're ready to paint. You'll be surprised at what you find. Then mask off the canopy and rear quarterlights. Paint the model using AeroMaster's RAF Dark Earth, Mid-Stone, and Azure Blue enamels. The AeroMaster paints are fairly thin straight from the jar, a factor that makes hand-brushing sometimes difficult. Even so, add a few drops of their thinner and the paints should go on smoothly with no problems. Paint the Mid-Stone first and let it dry about an hour. Then lightly drawn the camouflage pattern on the upper surface with a pencil. Spray the Dark Earth on free-hand using the pencil lines as a guide. Next, use the Azure Blue. Add a few drops of AeroMaster White to a fresh batch of Mid-Stone and then spray it into the middle of all the major panels and control surfaces using the

panel lines (not the rivets) as a guide. Repeat this process for the Dark Earth and Azure Blue. Add a couple of drops more of white to each color and spray them onto the fabric control surfaces to simulate the increased fade rate of fabric over metal. When the paint is dry, add a clear gloss coat. Paint the exhaust stacks Floquil Bronze.

Decals. We used Aeromaster decal sheet no. 48-057 "Wings Over the Sahara" for the model—an early P-40K (RAF Kittyhawk III) flown by Major D.B. Hauptfleisch, commanding officer of 2 Squadron of the Royal South African Air Force in North Africa. AeroMaster provides the standard RAF roundels and fin flashes, although some South African machines apparently flew with orange, instead of red, centers in the British roundels. Aeromaster has provided the orange centers, but acknowledges that it isn't known if this

particular aircraft had orange or red in the insignia. Well, it sure does look different. Our decals went on well over the gloss surface. Use a setting and solvent solution to get them to snuggle down, although they may not need it. When the decals are dry, give them a coat of Testor's Dullcote to seal them in and flatten the paint finish in preparation for weathering.

Weathering. Since the markings usually faded at a similar rate to the paint, apply a thin wash of Testor's Model Master Flat Gull Gray on the decals to tone them down. Apply a mix of black and brown watercolor (the cake type) to accent the control surfaces and a few of the major panel lines. Replicate paint chips with a combination of Flat Aluminum paint and a silver Berol Prismacolor pencil (available in any reasonably well-stocked arts and crafts store). The silver pencil's advantage is that it can be blended, in this case, with a Q-tip. Lightly color an area with the pencil and use the Q-tip to scrub the color into the paint. Use AeroMaster Tire Black to replicate soot from the guns and the exhausts. The Tire Black is actually a very dark gray and it looks better than straight black, which is too dark. Give the model a final coat of flat clear (fig. 12-12).

Final assembly. Add any remaining parts such as the tail wheel and doors. Paint the wingtip lights with Testor's Model Master Stop Light Red Metallic and Testor's Sapphire Blue (left and right respectively). Cement the canopy glass in place with Testor's Clear Parts Cement and rig the antennas with invisible thread and super glue them with an accelerator.

13
PACIFIC PINK

A P-40N almost out-of-the-box. Model by Glen Phillips

The ERTL P-40N was released soon after Mauve introduced their version. It consists of about 65 parts molded in a very soft, pale gray plastic. It is reasonably accurate and features finely engraved panel lines. Overall, the fit of the parts was good, but there were a few miscues which will be covered later. The kit includes decals for two aircraft, including the subject of this project.

The kit appears to have been set up to do early variants of the P-40. For one thing, to make the N in the kit, you must do a minor conversion by cutting out the rear of the cockpit. Very prominent internal engraved lines are provided for this purpose. Additionally, there is a mold seam around the rear of the fuselage, which indicates that perhaps a short tail is to be fitted. This

could have been for a standard P-40E, but maybe a broad tailed early K as well.

Begin construction with the cockpit, move to the fuselage and wings, and finish up by tacking on some sub-assemblies.

Cockpit. ERTL's cockpit effort is at least on par with Mauve's. In some cases it is better. ERTL has the separate side walls and rear bulkhead cemented to the cockpit floor. The relief on the side walls is far deeper and more technical-looking than Mauve's, but suffers from a few inaccuracies (fig. 13-1). Either use what is there or use the reference photos to improve the detail. In any event, paint carefully with Interior Green, follow with a black wash, and drybrush with Zinc Chromate to really pop out the details. Paint the electrical boxes and other gear flat black with

Fig. 13-1

red and yellow on some of the handles.

Assemble the cockpit floor and rear bulkhead as is, although a couple pieces of rod for the aileron and elevator control rods can really dress up the floor. Fill the ejection pin mark and sinkhole (if present) behind the headrest. They will be visible if you don't. Use Humbrol no. 56 Flat Aluminum to represent wear on the floor in front of the rudder pedals.

The seat is molded with engraved seat belts, which don't look that good in

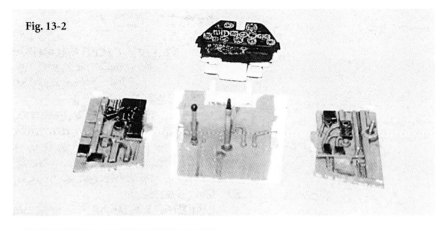
Fig. 13-2

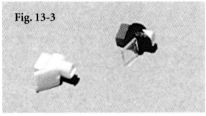
Fig. 13-3

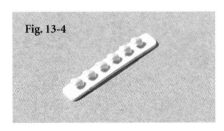
Fig. 13-4

Fuselage. Begin assembling the fuselage assembly by mounting the exhausts into the cowling side panels. ERTL provides the round tubular exhausts, but the subject of this project is Geronimo. This version is illustrated in Squadron/Signal Publications *P-40 Warhawk in Action* and it shows this aircraft with the flattened, flared exhausts more common on later P-40s. We didn't have a spare set of exhausts so we used the kit items. However, use a straight pin to make a small hole in the center of each exhaust (fig. 13-4). Paint the base of the exhausts flat black and firmly cement them into the panels. Otherwise, you may push them inside the cowl while handling the model later.

Clean up the filter elements at the front of the panels. These are small hinged (at the top) doors. A pair of cowling panel lines runs right through them. Fill these, sand them smooth, and drill out the filter holes (fig. 13-5).

Next, assemble and paint the radiator component. Use flat black on the radiator (part A7). Then drybrush it with Humbrol no. 53 Gunmetal. Paint the interior shroud parts (A4 and A5) AeroMaster Russian Light Blue.

Before cementing the fuselage shells together, remove the rear portion of the cockpit that sits under the rear quarterlights. Two very prominent V-shaped cuts are already engraved into the inside of the fuselage for this purpose. Just run a sharp no. 11 blade in the apex of the groove a few times and the pieces will snap cleanly away. Then cement the fuselage shells together and lightly clamp them after inserting the prop shaft and the completed radiator assembly. The fit on our model was adequate in that there were no major warps or differences in length and depth. Unlike Mauve, ERTL did neglect to offset the vertical fin 1.5 degrees to the left. Note that ERTL used a soft plastic in this kit, so go easy on the liquid cement. Otherwise, you'll have to clean up a lot of excess plastic bubbling out of the joints.

Next, add the left and right cowl panels. Here, we had a fit problem with our kit because the panels were too

1/48 scale. Scrape them off with a knife blade (not an easy task because of the seat contours) and replace them with masking tape painted off-white. Use Flat Aluminum to make the buckles.

The instrument panel (part K3) is rather odd. The main panel is very well done, but the sub-panel looks as if it was made by a different pattern maker. Below this, the rudder pedals and a blank central pedestal look as if they were done by a third pattern maker. Paint the two panels flat back, drybrush them with dark gray, and pick out the instruments with a white Eagle Prismacolor pencil. Pick out buttons, switches, and knobs in various colors using the reference photos as a guide (fig. 13-2). Clean up the rudder pedals, paint them Interior Green, and drybrush them with Flat Aluminum.

The kit gunsight (labeled a "bombsight" in the instructions) is molded with a solid plastic reflector glass. Trim this off and cement a piece of clear plastic in its place. Paint the sight flat black with a brown crash pad (fig. 13-3). Assemble all the cockpit components, except the gunsight, into a single unit and set it aside for later.

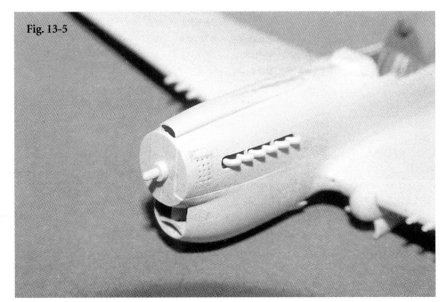
Fig. 13-5

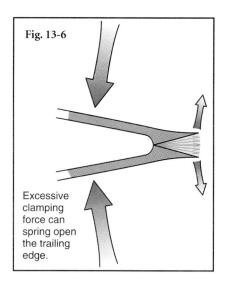

Fig. 13-6

Excessive clamping force can spring open the trailing edge.

small for the opening. The panels sit too far inside, creating a step all around. Bringing the panels out flush with the fuselage creates a gap all around. You will need to shim and trim carefully to make the parts fit as closely as possible. Remember, these seams are on a natural panel line, so if you lose any detail you must restore it.

Wings. Like Mauve, ERTL also boxed in the wheel wells, but they chose a slightly different route. The ribs and spars are molded as solid flanges on the inside of the lower wing panel (part B3). There are no lightening holes or any associated plumbing. Stringers are molded onto the inner surface of the upper wings—better than a blank hole. Paint the interior of the well Testor's Model Master Interior Green, wash it with thinned black paint, and drybrush it with Zinc Chromate.

Then dry-fit the wing panels together to check for burrs or gaps. When the fit is good, cement the parts together. Again, go easy on the cement, especially on the trailing edges. Too much cement there could easily distort the parts. Lightly clamp the wings for about 15 minutes or so, then remove the clamps (fig. 13-6). Add the left and right main gear covers. When the cement has dried, rub down all of the seams with a fine sanding stick and drill out the gun barrels. Also drill a hole in wing by the inner front corner of the landing gear pods for the brake line.

Now attach the wings to the fuselage. The fit on our model was very good. We only needed to do minor trimming or sanding along the fuselage wing root. Make sure you maintain the correct dihedral.

Detail parts. Add the rear cockpit shroud (part A6). It's listed as a gas tank in the instructions, but it's actually a cover for the gas tank. Paint the shroud either the external camouflage color (as the instructions suggest), or Interior Green. Both colors can be used interchangeably. Next, add the clear canopy (part E4) and fair it into the fuselage. Note the canopy panels seem to be a little shallow by about 1/8", slightly altering the look of the aircraft (fig. 13-7).

ERTL provides a separate cowl flap ring that is slightly opened. Just in case somebody wants to crawl under the model, add a pair of actuators using stretched sprue. Paint the interior of the flaps and the actuators Zinc Chromate (fig. 13-8).

Attach the pitot tube and antenna mast. Also add the drop tank braces if you're going to use the drop tank.

ERTL also forgot to include the drop tank's pylon, so make one from strip plastic and glue it to the bottom of the fuselage. Drill a small hole in the fuselage bottom just in front of the pylon for the drop tank feed pipe.

Remove the spinner parts from the sprue, clean off any burrs and tack them together with white glue or Kristal Kleer. Stick a paintbrush handle into the back to function as a handle for painting later.

Painting. Mask off the clear parts and remove any oily fingerprints and sanding dust before you paint. Spray the model with Xtra-Color X328, FS 10450, Light Tan for the Abu Dhabi Hawk Mk 63. This color is very close to what the aircraft in the Southwest Pacific area were painted. It's also very close to the box art, unlike the FS 33448 listed in the instruction sheet. That color is far too yellow. Add a bit of Xtra-Color White to the main color and spray it into the interior of all major panels and control surfaces. Add a little more white and spray once again onto the control surfaces. Most of the Xtra-Color paints for aircraft dry with a glossy finish. This paint takes at least 24 hours in a dust-free environment to dry. Now you don't need to apply a gloss coat prior to adding the decals. On the down side, Xtra-Color has an odor best described as unique. It'll take some getting used to (fig. 13-9).

Paint the underside Russian Light Blue because it is a close out-of-the-bottle match for FS 35550. Also add white to this color to pre-fade the interior of the panels and control surfaces. But go easy here. The fade rate on the

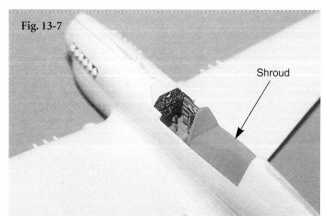

Fig. 13-7

Shroud

Fig. 13-8

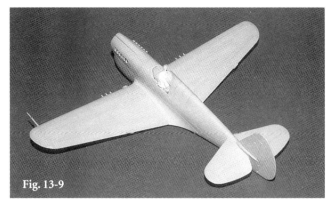
Fig. 13-9

Fig. 13-10

underside of an aircraft is less than that of the upper surfaces. The blue dries flat, so add a gloss coat when the paint is dry. Don't forget to paint the landing gear doors and any other ancillary items left off the model for the time being.

Decals. Use the kit decals, specifically Geronimo of the 45th FS, 15th FG. The decals seem to have a flat finish that makes them resistant to decal setting and solvent solutions. Reapply the solutions and the decals should go down with no further trouble. When the decals dry, seal them with a coat of flat clear (fig. 13-10).

Weathering. Spray the decals with a wash of light gray paint shot through the airbrush. This helps tone them down and matches their rate of weathering with the rest of the paint. Give control surfaces and major panels lines a wash of dark brown and black watercolor. Combine silver colored pencil and Flat Aluminum paint to replicate paint chipping. Keep in mind that most of the paint chips will be in the

area behind the prop. Spray a wash of dark gray through an airbrush to simulate gun and exhaust stains. Take a no. 2 brush, load about two-thirds of it with paint, and scrape it off in your airbrush's color cup. Do this about three or four times. Fill the color cup about half full of thinner. Blow a light stream of air back through the line and use bubbles to mix the paint and thinner. Remember to use a light stream of air. Too much pressure and you'll wind up with gray thinner all over your hand. While your particular airbrush setup may require some minor adjustments, that's the formula we used on this project. When finished, spray an additional coat of flat clear over the model (fig. 13-11).

Final assembly. The kit wheels left a little bit to be desired. The tires have a rectangular block tread pattern. Most P-40Ns flew without the wheel covers, leaving the spokes exposed. ERTL, however has provided the correct covered spokes for Geronimo. The wheel covers, however, stick out farther than

they should. Sand these down on a sanding stick and drill in the cover mounting bolts with a fine drill bit. Drill a hole for the brake line into the inner wheel hub (fig. 13-12).

Now tack on any remaining items left over from the construction phase. Add the landing gear struts, wheels and brake lines, the overly thick gear doors (make sure the tail wheel well doors splay outward rather than hang straight down), gunsight, canopy parts, and the propeller and landing light.

Drill a small hole in the upper forward portion of the tank. Insert a piece of copper wire, paint it flat black, insert it into the hole and the hole in the bottom of the fuselage to replicate the fuel feed line. That completes the project (fig. 13-13).

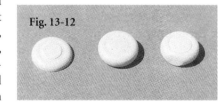
Fig. 13-12

Fig. 13-11

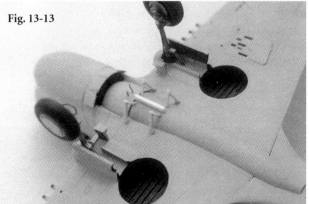
Fig. 13-13

14
LAST OF THE LINE

A P-40N of the 49th Fighter Group. Model by Kevin Hjermstad

The Mauve P-40N is a good representation of the improvements in the mold maker's art. Overall, the kit has a good fit, finely engraved panel lines, individual exhaust stacks, and a detailed, though simplified, cockpit. Built straight out of the box it is a fine example of how far model making has come.

We used very little filler during construction, although there was a small gap in the right wing root and there was a step on the trailing edge between the wing and fuselage. The instrument panel didn't fit inside the fuselage very well, but it is beautifully engraved. Overall, it's a great-looking kit, and more importantly a great-fitting kit.

Cockpit. Use the True Details P-40N resin cockpit interior set (fig. 14-1) to replace the stock kit interior. The resin kit is a real work of art. All the detail you could ask for is cast into those

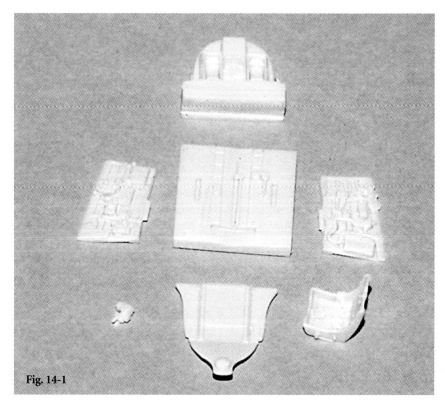

Fig. 14-1

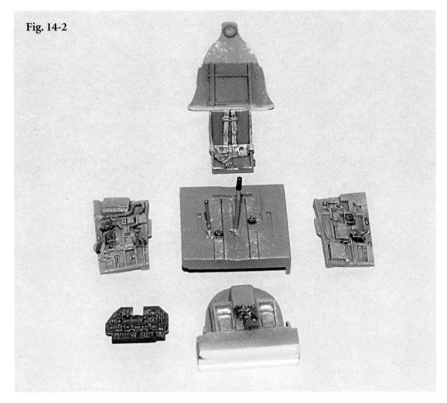

Fig. 14-2

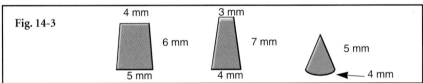

Fig. 14-3

4 mm · 6 mm · 5 mm
3 mm · 7 mm · 4 mm
5 mm · 4 mm

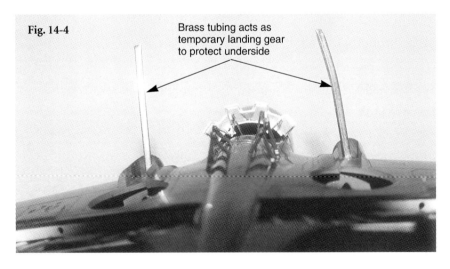

Fig. 14-4

Brass tubing acts as temporary landing gear to protect underside

that came with the replacement cockpit. They contain FS-595A color references to help you with color selection. Paint the cockpit Gunze Sangyo no. 58 Interior Green with no. 12 Flat Black radio boxes, throttle quadrant, control panels, etc.

Wash the cockpit with thinned raw umber oil paint and drybrush it with Interior Green mixed with white oil paint. Pick out other items in red, brown, and black. Paint the seat belts khaki and wash them with the raw umber. Paint the buckles silver.

Paint the instrument panel flat black and drybrush it with gray oil paint. Pick out individual dials with white oil paint. After the dials dry, apply drops of Kristal Kleer with a toothpick to simulate instrument panel glass. Create the appearance of chipped paint in the cockpit interior with a mixture of raw umber oil paint and silver enamel. Brush and scrub the mixture where there was handling and foot traffic. Then spray the entire assembly, except the instrument panel, with Testor's Dullcote (fig. 14-2).

Fuselage. Add detail to the Fuselage by adding cowl flaps and drilling out the upper cowl air intake. Assemble the fuselage according to the instructions, paying close attention to the radiator intake assembly. After cementing, we had to fill a small seam on the upper air intake.

After the fuselage halves are cemented together and the seams removed, jockey the kit instrument panel into position. The fit was very poor on our kit—so poor, in fact, that it seems to have been an afterthought. The upper shape of the panel bears no relationship at all to the inner surface of the instrument panel shroud. Curve the inner surface of the fuselage to help fit the panel as best as possible, secure it with super glue.

Replace the kit cowl flaps with new ones constructed from .010" styrene. Cut four triangular pieces to form the outer portion of the cowl. Then make four more, slightly smaller than the first ones. Glue them together into four sub-assemblies. Attach each to the assembled fuselage with super glue and let it

pieces. The resin kit does not include an instrument panel, but the one in the Mauve kit is the best part of that kit's interior. This is all fine, but we'll tell you how to add a few more details to the cockpit set.

Remove the resin carriers from the pieces by scribing them along their bases until they are paper thin. Then

cut them off with an X-acto knife and finish them off with sanding sticks. Cut off thicker parts with a razor saw.

The kidney armor plate was missing from right side of our kit. Cut one out of .010" sheet plastic and fit it in place. Add the gunsight reflector glass with clear .010" styrene.

Follow the painting instructions

dry in position. Cut three small triangles with circular bottoms from .010" sheet and add them in-between the first flap assemblies. Also attach these with super glue (fig. 14-3). Cut the actuators to a basic shape then carve them down further with needle files to give them a delicate appearance. After you attach the actuators use pieces of stretched sprue to simulate the control rods that drew the cowl open and closed (fig. 14-4). The upper engine cowl has a perforated filter cover. Drill the holes out with a no. 71 bit.

Wings. Add new flaps using Kendall Model Company's P-40 Control Surfaces set. First, cut the kit flaps out of the lower wing using a scriber. Clean up the edges with a fine file and sanding stick. Cut out a piece of .010" sheet plastic and fit it into the flap well under the fuselage. This piece represents the inner surface of the upper wing (fig. 14-5). Cut another long strip of .010" strip and use it to box in the front of the flap well. Cement all of these in place with liquid cement and let them dry.

Next, cut some .040" x .040" Evergreen strip to represent the stringers in the well bay. Cut another piece of .010" styrene sheet into a square and drill it with a series of round and oval holes to represent the gusset plate. Lastly, add small pieces to the inside edges of the flap well (fig. 14-6). Don't try to duplicate every rib and actuator in the flap well, just create a general imitation of what is located in the well. Remove the resin flap pieces from their runners with a razor saw. Paint them with the

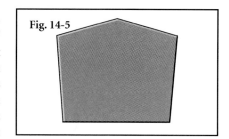

Fig. 14-5

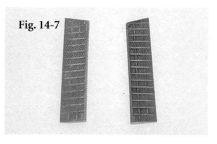

Fig. 14-7

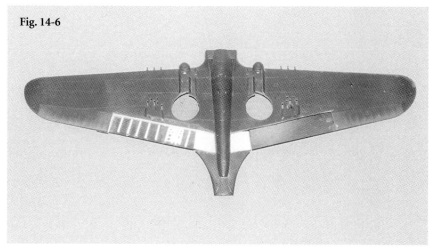

Fig. 14-6

rest of the airframe and attach them towards the end of the model's assembly (fig. 14-7).

Drill out the kit gun barrels with a no. 79 bit. These can also be substituted with hypodermic tubing.

Add detail to the wheel wells with copper wire from a motor armature. The wire represents the hydraulic lines in the wheel wells. Paint the wells with Testor's Model Master Zinc Chromate,

wash them with burnt sienna oil paint, and drybrush them.

Use craft wire to simulate the brake hoses on the aircraft struts. Use model railroad eyelets as hose retainers on the back of the struts. Drill a hole in the brake hub and attach the hose there. Then loop the hose up the back side of the strut through the eyelets and into another hole in the wing.

Assemble and flatten the wheels

Fig. 14-8

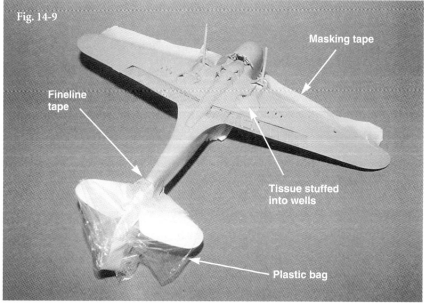

Fig. 14-9

Masking tape

Fineline tape

Tissue stuffed into wells

Plastic bag

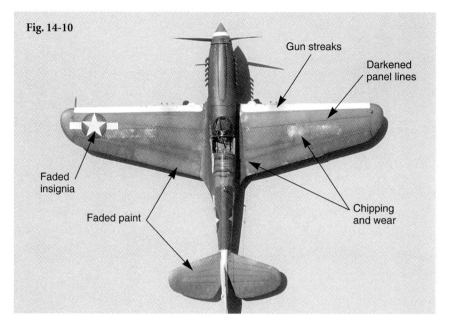

Fig. 14-10

Gun streaks

Darkened panel lines

Faded insignia

Faded paint

Chipping and wear

on a 75-watt light bulb to soften the plastic. Then press the tire onto a piece of glass (fig. 14-8). Paint the struts and wheel hubs with Testor's Aluminum and wash them with raw umber oil paint. Don't attach the wheels and struts until later. Drill air inlets in the leading edge of the wing root with a no. 60 bit.

The wings, cockpit, and fuselage are now assembled. Add the rear section of the auxiliary gas tank cover and paint it Interior Green. Then wash and drybrush it. Use a Squadron vacu-formed canopy because it fits better on the rear section than the kit canopy. Attach the rear canopy with watch-crystal cement and let it dry. Fill the seam with super glue and sand it smooth. Mask off the canopy and spray it Interior Green to match the rest of the interior. Leave the canopy mask on and seal off the cockpit with drafting tape for the upcoming application of paint.

Painting. Paint the entire airframe with Testor's Model Master Primer. Prime the aircraft because it is molded in dark green plastic and has a white tail fin. This gives the paint an even base so there is no burn through, especially with the white tail section.

Well, nothing gets a rousing debate going amongst modelers like talking color schemes. There are as many opinions about which colors are right as there are people who model

aircraft. We mention this because you must choose a decal sheet now.

This aircraft is a P-40N flown by Lt. Joel B. Paris of the 49th Fighter Group in the Southwest Pacific. A Three Guys decal sheet no. TGR-48010 shows Paris's aircraft with olive drab upper surfaces over neutral gray, with white leading edges and tail section (except the upper surfaces of the horizontal stabilizer, which were olive drab). There seems to be some controversy over the colors used on the aircraft, so for simplicity's sake we went with the Three Guys scheme.

Mask the canopies with a medical waterproof tape called Blenderm. Use a new no. 11 X-acto to cut out the canopy framing. Spray the canopies Interior Green before applying the topside color.

First spray Floquil Reefer White over the tail assembly, spinner, and wing leading edges. Unlike many white paints on the market, this color has good opacity and excellent coverage. Other white paints require many coats and still let the underlying color bleed through.

After this dries, mask off the tail section with 3M Fineline tape. Use a plastic sandwich bag as a mask for the rest of the elevator and rudder assembly. Mask off the leading edges of the wings as well for the upcoming color coats. Then spray the edges of the mask

with white to seal them and provide a clean edge (fig. 14-9).

Apply Gunze Sangyo's Neutral Gray no. 53 to the lower fuselage, wings, and flaps. After this dries, mask off the lower fuselage with Fineline tape and 1" drafting tape below that to protect from overspray. Before applying the olive drab, seal the edges of the demarcation line with another coat of neutral gray.

Spray Gunze Sangyo Olive Drab no. 52 over the entire aircraft top side and let it dry. After the paint dries, remove all the masks except those on the canopies. Lastly, mask off the lower elevator and the rudder so the Olive Drab can be applied to the upper surfaces of the elevators.

After the aircraft paint cures for a day, begin the process of fading the aircraft paint. Fade the undersides first. Mix a small amount of white into the neutral gray. The approximate ratio is about 70 percent neutral gray to 30 percent white. Tint the paint just enough to lighten the base color but not to create a sharp contrast. Practice spraying it on some scrap plastic to get a feel for it. Start by filling in all the areas between the panel lines, lightening the center but leaving the edges the base color. Work your way down the airframe, from nose to tail and out to the wing tips. If the contrast appears too stark, even out the surface by spraying the base color back over the model to blend it down.

Apply the same method to the top of the aircraft, fading the entire upper surface. You might want to fade the fabric-covered surfaces a little more because these tended to fade faster than the aluminum surfaces, especially in the hot Pacific sun.

Mask off the spinner with Fineline tape for the blue squadron marking. Spray Tamiya's no. X-F 8 Flat Blue over the spinner assembly. Then overspray it with a lightened mixture made with no. X-F 2 Flat White and Flat Blue. This will make the spinner look weather-beaten. Paint the prop blades flat black with yellow prop tips. Drybrush them with Testor's Dark Gray enamel.

Give the airframe two coats of Testor's Glosscote and let it dry for 24 hours in preparation for the application of the decals.

Decals. As stated before, use the decal sheet from Three Guys Replicas. The decals should go on with no trouble. Apply them with Micro-Sol and Micro-Set. After they dry, inspect them for air bubbles. If you find any, pierce them and apply more Micro-Set. Let them dry for 24 hours before you begin the weathering process.

After all the decals are in place, give the model 2 to 3 light, misty coats of Testor's Dullcote. After it dries make sure the aircraft appears as one unified piece. Flat coats seem to bring all your painting efforts together. Don't forget to coat the canopy framing too.

Weathering (fig. 14-10). Weathering an aircraft model is a touchy subject for some people. Ultimately, it boils down to a matter of personal preference. Many aircraft, especially those fighting in extreme climates, look weather-beaten. Many units also fought at the end of a very long, and often tenuous, supply line. Keeping the aircraft pretty was secondary in importance to combat readiness. Adding weathering to an aircraft, be it heavy or light, adds to the realism and helps enhance the finished model.

Begin the weathering process of fading the paint by lightening it on the top and bottom sides of the airframe. Then accent the panel lines with washes of oil paint. Mix up burnt umber oil paint with a product called Turpinoid (this is a turpentine substitute that doesn't smell as much). You want tinted thinner, not thinned paint. Use a brush no. 00 to flow the mixture into all the recessed panel lines. If some slops out, don't worry. Use an old T-shirt dampened in Turpinoid to wipe it down. Work in small areas at a time and let it set for about 10 minutes. Then wipe it down with the dampened rag. If needed, lightly rescribed the panel lines to get the wash to settle in the recesses.

Paint chips usually occur around the aircraft leading edges and areas hit by the prop wash. Paint usually gets scuffed around areas of foot traffic,

Fig. 14-11

Fig. 14-12

maintenance access doors, cockpit floors, and walkways. Use a mixture of raw umber oil paint and Testor's Silver to create paint chips. There are no mixing formulas—just blend them together on an index card until the look is right: not too brown and not a stark silver. Using a small-tipped brush, dab the mixture around the plane until you are satisfied. To create a scuffed-paint effect, blend the paint-chip mixture into the aircraft with a Q-tip cotton swab.

Oil and hydraulic stains are simulated with raw umber oil paint straight out of the tube. Take a small brush and load the end with a dab of paint and place it where you want the stain to begin. Then, wipe the spot backwards toward the tail, following the flow of air. Do only a few of these—you don't want it to look as if a hydraulic line has just burst.

Exhaust stains and powder residue are made using pastel chalk. Use a mixture of black and gray for the exhaust.

Scrape the pastel sticks and blend them together in the crease of a folded 3 x 5 card. Apply the chalk mixture with a brush onto and around the exhausts and streak them down the fuselage. Apply the gun residue the same way, except mix dark brown into the black instead of gray. Make these streaks along the wings although sometimes they are shorter than exhaust streaks. Don't forget the shell ejector ports.

Treat the decals to a little weathering as well. Give them a subtle coat of Gunze Sangyo no. 61 IJN Light Gray. Spray a light tint on top of all the decals to reduce their stark brilliance on the weathered aircraft. You must have a very light touch with the airbrush or you will have a nice Light Gray blob of paint on your wing obscuring what used to be a nice decal. Again, practice on scrap plastic before spraying the finished model.

Final assembly. At this point, attach all remaining parts and accessories to the aircraft: the landing gear and

Fig. 14-13

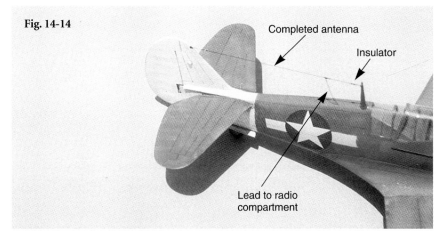

Fig. 14-14

Completed antenna

Insulator

Lead to radio compartment

Mount the struts in place and glue the brake hoses into small holes in the wheel well. Attach the wheels, making sure the flat spots on the tires are flat on the ground. Paint the gear doors along with the rest of the aircraft and insert them in place with super glue. Paint them neutral gray outside and Testor's Zinc Chromate inside.

What about those flaps? They are one of the last items to be put on so they would not get knocked off during construction. Mount them into the wells with super glue and crack them open. Do not open them all the way because the detail was to be a representation not a duplication of the actual item (figs. 14-11 and 14-12).

Lastly, attach an antenna wire using tailor's thread (fig. 14-13). This is a clear, small-diameter thread that is perfect for model aircraft. Drill a hole in the airframe where you want the antenna. Pool some super glue in a bottle cap and dip an end of the thread into the glue. Place the super-glued end into the hole and hit it with a dollop of super glue accelerator. As soon as that end is dry, pull the other end taut and dip and place the wire in the other hole. Hit this with accelerator. Now you have a nice, taut antenna wire.

Dab a small drop of paint at the ends of the wire to cover the small drilled hole. The antenna can be left clear or painted black. Apply Kristal Kleer with a toothpick or small brush on the ends to simulate insulators (fig. 14-14).

wheels, gear doors, tail wheel, and drop tank. You can put a flat coat on these before or after they are attached.

With the aircraft inverted, attach the underside components. Mount a small wire, painted black to represent the fuel hose, in the top of the drop tank. Drill a corresponding hole in the pylon underneath. Use the kit sway braces, although these require some maneuvering because they don't fit very well.

INDEX

airbrushes, 21
assembly, basic, 22
    P-40E, 24, 60
    P-40K, 73

brushes, 20

cockpit
    P-40B, 49, 53
    P-40E, 44, 60
    P-40F, 68
    P-40K, 74
    P-40N, 27, 78, 82
conversion
    P-40F, 67
    P-40K, 73
    parts, preparing
        P-40B, 53
        P-40F, 67

decals, 23
    P-40B, 51
    P-40E, 46, 63
    P-40F, 71
    P-40K, 77
    P-40N, 31, 81, 86
details, 11
detail parts
    P-40B, 51, 56
    P-40E, 62
    P-40F, 69
    P-40K, 75
    P-40N, 29, 80

ERTL P-40N, 39, 78

fillers, 20
final assembly
    P-40B, 52, 59
    P-40E, 26, 65
    P-40F, 71
    P-40K, 77
    P-40N, 31, 81, 86
final finishing, P-40E, 46
flat coats, 23
fuselage
    P-40B, 50, 54
    P-40E, 45, 61
    P-40F, 69
    P-40K, 74
    P-40N, 28, 79, 83

Hasegawa
    P-40E, 24, 33, 44
    P-40N, 27, 33

masking, 23
Mauve
    P-40M (basis of conversion
        to P-40F), 37, 67
    P-40N, 39, 82
Monogram
    P-40B, 34, 35, 48
    P-40E, 36, 60

Otaki
    P-40E, 73
    P-40K, 38

P-40
    colors and markings, 32
    details, 11
    development, 6
P-40B, 48, 53
    cockpit, 49, 53
    conversion parts, 53
    decals, 51
    detail parts, 51, 56
    development, 6
    final assembly, 52, 59
    fuselage, 50, 54
    Monogram kit, 34, 35
    painting, 51, 58
    weathering, 51, 59
    wings, 50, 55
P-40C, 6
P-40D/E, 7
P-40E, 24, 44, 60
    assembly, 24, 60
    cockpit, 44, 60
    decals, 46, 63
    detail parts, 62
    final assembly, 26, 65
    final finishing, 46
    fuselage, 45, 61
    Hasegawa kit, 33
    Monogram kit, 36
    painting, 25, 45, 62
    weathering, 46, 64
    wings, 45, 62
P-40F, 37, 67
    cockpit, 68
    conversion parts, 67
    decals, 71
    detail parts, 70
    development, 7
    final assembly, 71
    fuselage, 69
    painting, 70
    weathering, 71
P-40K, 73
    assembly, 73

    cockpit, 74
    decals, 77
    detail parts, 75
    development, 8
    final assembly, 77
    fuselage, 74
    Otaki kit, 38
    painting, 76
    weathering, 77
    wings, 75
P-40L, 9
P-40M, 10
P-40N, 27, 78, 82
    cockpit, 27, 78, 82
    decals, 31, 81, 86
    detail parts, 29, 80
    development, 10
    ERTL kit, 39
    final assembly, 31, 81, 86
    fuselage, 28, 79, 83
    Hasegawa kit, 33
    Mauve kit, 39
    painting, 29, 80, 85
    weathering, 31, 81, 86
    wings, 28, 80, 84
painting, 20, 22
    P-40B, 51, 58
    P-40E, 25, 45, 62
    P-40F, 70
    P-40K, 76
    P-40N, 29, 80, 85

seams, 21

techniques, basic, 21
tools, 20

weathering, 23
    P-40B, 51, 59
    P-40E, 46, 64
    P-40F, 71
    P-40K, 77
    P-40N, 31, 81, 86
wings
    P-40B, 50, 55
    P-40E, 45, 62
    P-40K, 75
    P-40N, 28, 80, 84

XP-40
    colors, 38
    development, 5
XP-40Q, 10